A Business Tale

A Story of Ethics, Choices, Success— and a Very Large Rabbit

Marianne M. Jennings

AMACOM

American Management Association
New York • Atlanta • Brussels • Buenos Aires • Chicago• London • Mexico City
San Francisco • Shanghai • Tokyo • Toronto • Washington, D.C.

Library of Congress Cataloging-in-Publication Data

Jennings, Marianne.
  A business tale : a story of ethics, choices, success—and a very large rabbit / Marianne M. Jennings.
      p. cm.
Includes bibliographical references and index.
  ISBN 0-8144-7197-8
  1. Business ethics—Fiction. 2. Choice (Psychology)—Fiction. 3. Success in business—Fiction. I. Title.

PS3610.E56B87 2003
813'.6—dc21   2003006175

Printing number

10 9 8 7 6 5 4 3 2 1

For all the pookas in my life who have ever felt outrage:
Faith, family, friends, and students

Marianne M. Jennings is the author of:

Business Ethics: Case Studies and Selected Readings,
    Fourth Edition (2002)

Business: Its Legal, Ethical, and Global Environment,
    Sixth Edition (2002)

Real Estate Law, Sixth Edition (2001)

Nobody Fixes Real Carrot Sticks Anymore (1994)

Avoiding and Surviving Lawsuits: The Executive
    Guide to Strategic Legal Planning for Business (1989)

She is also the coauthor of:

Business Law and the Regulatory Environment:
    Cases and Principles, 15th Edition (2003)

Building a Business Through Good Times and Bad: Lessons
    from 15 Companies, Each with a Century of Dividends (2002)

Business Law and the Legal Environment, 18th Edition (2002)

Business Strategy for the Political Arena (1984)

Contents

Foreword

I've been as frustrated as the next person with the reality that life and people just aren't always fair, the good guys don't always win, goodness doesn't always win out, the best (wo)man doesn't always get the job, honesty isn't always the winning policy, and noble convictions don't always pay off; nor does doing the right thing guarantee success, accolades, or even appreciation, much less a brass ring.

In fact, "doing the right thing" will often put you in a risky position. You could lose position, power, material success—or your very life. Why? Because in the real world there is a constant battle between good and evil—and evil has no shame, no limits, no rules, and largely, no fear. Against that formula many people crumble, acquiesce, and even abdicate their values. After all, there are profits to be made, children to be sent to private school, job opportunities too good to lose, connections to be made, perks to enjoy, an ego to satisfy, competitions to be won, vacations and lovely homes to be had—and it seems that bending ethical rules or points of law is what everybody has to do if they want to be competitive.

Whew! Difficult choices. Why would you ever choose to buck the system and do the right thing, the ethical thing, when it's so clear that you could pay a real and depressing price? Why would you choose to sacrifice profits, opportunities, and power for some noble ideal of personal and professional ethics and morality that clearly isn't shared by those in your sphere? What's really wrong with not speaking up for what or who is right if it's going to hurt you? What's really wrong with doing things you don't believe in to keep and grow your job? What's really wrong with sucking up or selling out when you're only doing so to get yourself in a better position? What's really wrong with making quality and service secondary to profit when there are supervisors to please and stockholders to satisfy?

These are good questions. These are questions you'll face in one form or other just about every day of your personal and professional life. When the noble, idealistic convictions you were taught as a child come into conflict with your career goals, opportunities, and unforeseen circumstances, one very important thing happens: you come face-to-face with the truth of who you really are.

When you were a child you had dreams of what you'd do when you grew up. Don't dismiss these dreams as silly, unrealistic fantasies. In your childhood dreams you were idealistic and altruistic. Your childhood dreams were directed toward a noble goal representing your special gift. Is the world ever better off when these dreams are set aside as naïve, impractical, unrealistic, or foolishly innocent? Is it worth it to sacrifice being a good person in order to "do well"? Does "what" you are matter more to you than "who" you are?

Too many people answer "yes" to these questions. Many are willing to sacrifice the "good person" role for that of the most powerful, most known, most rich, most liked, most feared, or most (superficially) beloved. There is a tremendous amount of societal pressure to do just that, and currently there is also a paucity of societal shame, rejection, or punishment of wrongdoers.

Why then would any reasonable, sane person refrain from cutting that corner if they could get away with it? For many, the answer is in their upbringing: They just can't make themselves break the rules and disappoint or shame their parents. For others, the answer is that they believe it would be an affront to God. For still others it is as simple as that they find that success without integrity brings no joy.

Success and possessions without integrity frankly are just a big letdown. To avoid that letdown feeling, many people compulsively grab for more and more and more—only to feel let down time after time. That's when some turn to drugs, alcohol, or compulsive sex in order to push away that letdown feeling.

The letdown is due to your soul and psyche not being satisfied. Those elements of your being can be ignored—but ultimately not denied. When your goals or motivations are not worthy, when your tactics are not worthy of your goals, when your end result has no true nobility involved, your soul and psyche are starved of pride and true satisfaction. In addition, you will not be a happy person.

There is no happiness in a life scraped clean of integrity, morality, and ethics; life eventually feels meaningless.

As I prefaced my book *How Could You Do That?! The Abdication of Character, Courage, and Conscience:* "I don't wonder that so many people search blindly for the 'meaning of life.' What they don't seem to understand is that life does not have meaning through mere existence or acquisition or fun. The meaning of life is inherent in the connections we make to others through honor and obligation."

I'll leave you with this "gimmick" I use with callers on my radio program who are struggling with a moral/ethical dilemma after they've rummaged unsatisfyingly through their lists of pros and cons in order to formulate a decision. It involves a Dickens moment in which I become the Ghost of Christmas Future. I tell them that, "By the power vested in me because of this radio program I can project you twenty years into your own future and you can view yourself in live action as you are today. You get to watch yourself as you make this choice today. What do you want to see that will make you *proud?*"

Then, as the Nike commercial says, "Just do it."

Well, I'll always be proud of writing the foreword for Professor Marianne Jennings's wonderful book about business ethics. Considering recent scandals of corporate greed and corruption, polls showing that high-school honors seniors believe cheating is one of many acceptable tools, and a general societal decline in valuing sacrifice, spirituality, and integrity (voting instead for acquisition, power, and self-actualization) this book ought to be considered a *must-read* in every classroom, every office, and every home.

Dr. Laura C. Schlessinger
Author and internationally
syndicated radio talk-show host

Acknowledgments

I am the product of family, friends and faith. This book comes from me, but how can it be separated from these? I have simply written what they have taught me for a lifetime. So, I thank my many co-authors in this all-too-brief acknowledgment.

I have been blessed with goodly parents who taught me of right and wrong and added the lesson of God first, others second, and putting yourself last. But they surely deserve first place here.

I have also been blessed with a husband whose DNA matches when it comes to questions of right and wrong. We complete each other's sentences as we analyze everything from movies to our children's behavior and accompanying punishments to our rights under the Second Amendment. I'd call him my soul mate, but we both hate that notion. Nonetheless, our two souls have produced four terrific children who continue to be tolerant of a mother who perhaps has spent too much time at the computer. Terry, Sarah, Claire, Sam, and John, thanks for the love, support, quiet, and inspiration via chaos.

I also had a Chekov sort of life with three sisters who remain loyal to that unifying set of values our parents gave us. Janice, Cynthia, and Jennifer have been there for each moment of joy and crisis with love, advice, and plenty of good humor. Their wit is in this fable.

I have had one additional family blessing—an extended family who took an interest in my work and remained regular correspondents. For my late Uncle Ed, a belated thank you for teaching me about work ethic. And for my dear Uncle Alex, for thinking better of me than I deserve.

I would never have written a fable had it not been for my agents Greg Dinkin and Frank Scatoni of Venture Literary. These two gentlemen taught me using a carrot, and not a stick. The metaphor on rabbits continues. Greg held a special place in my heart and mind long before he was an agent because he had been my student. He was an engaged, thinking, and conscientious student who took business ethics to heart and lives it.

And, oh, my students. How they have taught me. And how they continue to share with me their experiences and challenges. And how they honor me by returning to seek my advice and input when they face the inevitable dilemmas of their professional lives.

There are those in business who have also taught me by example and by honoring me with their time for discussions of the ethical issues that challenge businesses and employees. To Mark DeMichele, the officers of Hy-Vee Foods, Tim Day, and others who continue to show me character is alive and well in business—my gratitude and respect.

There are so many colleagues over the years who have debated, questioned, analyzed, and refined my thoughts. Professors Steve Happel, Bruce Childers, Lohnie Boggs, David Lynch, Peter Reiss, Phil Reckers, John Norton, Linda Christianson, and Wayne Baty, along with my friends, Peter Baird and John Entine, have all been influences with their lives and kind words. And they have been supportive colleagues for the views of one who has become a radical in her field for her refusal to accept moral relativism.

And there are the friends whose lives are exemplars, Marianne Alcorn, Judith Roland, Jackie Wilcock, Diane and Hoke Holyoak, Pat Leider, Tina Terry, Ann McClellan, Rich Rosen, Kelly Kimble, and Jeanette and Harold Debbi. Little did they know I studied them to become better.

I am grateful to Ellen Kadin, my editor, for her recognition of Edgar's charm and the importance of his tale. I appreciate Erika Spelman's work and attention to detail.

I'm grateful for all who have fired me over the years because of my standards. They helped me understand what was important. Despite my gratitude, I won't name them here. My faith has taught me to heed the words of St. Paul: "We are troubled on every side, yet not distressed; we are perplexed, but not in despair. Persecuted, but not forsaken; cast down, but not destroyed."

This is a rough road, this ethics thing. It would be nice to have Ari, the pooka, along for the ride. But I believe he has a few apostles he has sent my way. And I am enormously grateful for their very visible presence in my life and this book.

*"What is right is right, even if no one is doing it.
What is wrong is wrong, even if everyone is doing it."*
—Source unknown

*"The weakest of all weak things is a virtue that has
not been tested in the fire."*
—Mark Twain

Introduction
The Story Behind *A Business Tale*

I took no joy in the ethical and financial collapses of Enron, WorldCom, Tyco, and Adelphia and the resulting losses to shareholders and employees. Even seeing Martha Stewart under the federal prosecutorial microscope has been no fun. (Well, perhaps there's a part of me that would enjoy seeing Bernie Ebbers, Jeff Skilling, and Andrew Fastow sentenced to heavy labor or Hades. And there would be a certain delicious irony in Martha coping with minimum security's powdered potatoes and green Jell-O for three to five years.)

Still, there is a part of me that rejoices because that part wants to shout, "I told you so!" after more than twenty years of enjoying pats on the head for my efforts to teach business ethics, but being secretly tossed aside by faculty and students who consider my material "soft," and not terribly important for the future titans of America who are rewarded for increasing shareholder value at any cost. But as much noise as I made and as many demands as I made for outrage, folks just never quite got what I have been saying for twenty years: *building shareholder value and practicing sound ethics are one and the same.*

1

Finance theories taught students that their only ethical obligation was to maximize shareholder value. I taught the same to *my* students. However, our approaches were slightly different. The finance profs taught them how to manage earnings; the accounting profs taught them how to spin debt off the books; and I taught them that those practices pushed legal and ethical limits and helped no one in the long run. I just never had a model for calculating the financial risk of pushing those limits.

Enron, Adelphia, WorldCom, Tyco, Kmart, and an ongoing list of companies experiencing difficulties, issuing earnings restatements, and grappling with years of less-than-honest financials, have quantified the value of ethics even beyond my wildest dreams. Fiction could not have brought a better scenario and backdrop for teaching the importance of ethics. Business has always been about making money, but so has business ethics. You can't make money in the long run without ethics. Until these collapses that had an impact on virtually everyone from shareholders to employees and back to suppliers and customers, no one could quantify the costs of poor ethical choices. Now we can. On January 14, 2001, Enron's share price was $83. Exactly one year later, on January 14, 2002, following earnings restatements, document shredding, and an SEC and Justice Department filled with wrath and investigations, Enron's share price was $0.14. One day in October 2001, shareholders were told that in addition to the $586 million restatement of earnings, they would have to take a $1.2 billion reduction in equity. WorldCom's shareholders lost $3.5 billion in earnings in one restatement. That slight accounting glitch meant they really had no earnings in the company for three years. And that was only the beginning. By the end of 2002, WorldCom's restatements of income would reach over $9 billion. As one of my colleagues has said, investing $1,000 in Enron or WorldCom would leave you with about $5 today. You would have been better off putting $1,000 in the purchase of beer and recycling the cans, thereby netting about $50.

Ethics matter even when it comes to the personal lives of managers. When an indictment against former Tyco CEO Dennis Kozlowski for sales tax evasion on multimillion-dollar art transactions was announced, the market took a 200-plus point dive. Already reeling from questions about Tyco's finances, investors became more nervous about trustworthiness of companies in general. Jack Welch's postretirement package and the revelations in his divorce case about his perks forced him to the airways to stop slippage in GE stock. Just the hint that Martha Stewart might have engaged in earth-toned insider trading in a company other than her own, sent her Omnimedia stock sliding 31 percent.

The accounting issues are not the only source of ethics' quantification. On the product liability front, a jury handed down a $4.8 billion verdict (reduced on appeal to a mere $1.2 billion) in a case involving the position of the gas tank in General Motors' Malibu. Two internal memos took the jury aback. One was from a young engineer who worried about the danger of the position of the gas tank. Another was from a lawyer reviewing the young engineer's memo who recommended that no one be allowed anywhere near the engineer or the memo.

My devotion to the field of ethics began innocently enough—and it is only appropriate that devotion to a field such as ethics be fraught with innocence. Somehow devotion to ethics for Machiavellian reasons lacks sincerity. Gordon Gekko (Michael Douglas) of *Wall Street* told us, "Greed, for lack of a better word, is good." This was one Oliver Stone movie that provided more than a grassy knoll overstatement. Despite the film's ending, Gordon Gekko's dialogue became the credo of numerous businesspeople.

It was during this era of fictional and real tycoons (like Ivan Boesky) that this not-so-young-professor looked over her students' responses to legal, moral, and ethical dilemmas and had an awakening. My reaction to the musings of my graduate students in business when we discussed the ethics of making money was profound: "These kids are going to end up in prison."

Therein was the innocent birth of my devotion to the field of business ethics. The recognition that students lack character and ethics these days was the inspiration for Vin Diesel and the script of *Dude, Where's My Car?*—but it's not exactly material for a course or a book. The challenge lies in retraining those minds, formulated in a secular world, to understand *why* ethics is important in business and life, and *how* to go about being ethical. My challenge was great, given that I teach in a state-funded institution of higher learning that punishes professors who make reference to religion by burning them at the stake (and those are the tenured ones).

Secular ethics…is it possible? Is it possible to teach ethics to adults? Is it possible to train minds that the finance professors and economists have polluted with notions that the "ethical" responsibility of an executive is to do *whatever it takes* to increase shareholder value? Is it possible to tout "the right thing to do" to folks who speak in Betas and throw around EBITDAs that could knock the wind out of Warren Buffett's sails? Is there any hope left out there post–Enron, WorldCom, Tyco, and Adelphia and this era of one bankruptcy after another becoming the largest bankruptcy in the history of the United States? (How do we even know whether their claim to the largest bankruptcy ever is true? Their numbers on everything else have been fabricated from the halls of *pro forma* to the shores of the Cayman Islands.)

The answer, in a word, is yes. Of course it is possible to help adults understand why ethics is important in their lives and work. *Who*

Moved My Cheese has proven that readers like to be engaged in a story, as simple as it might seem. And as *Fish!* has shown, the mantra of "show, don't tell" applies to business books. *A Business Tale* is the story of four people in business. Edgar is shadowed by an invisible "pooka" that keeps him on his ethical toes and prevents him from moving out of his studio apartment or advancing up the corporate ladder. Meanwhile, Edgar's friends—Drew, Heather, and Steve—who don't have the burden of an ethical pooka, are striking it rich.

∷

This is a tale that uses Aesop's "The Tortoise and the Hare" as its framework and details the journey of these four businesspeople, showing that neither life nor business is a sprint, it's a marathon—and that those who play by the rules really do win in the long run. The result is a fable that illustrates the importance of ethics in business.

The notion of a "pooka" comes from Mary Chase's Pulitzer Prize–winning play, *Harvey*, which was made into a movie in 1950, featuring Jimmy Stewart as Elwood P. Dowd, the lead character. Elwood is a bright fellow who has the good fortune of being accompanied by a "pooka." A pooka is a mischievous spirit, generally in the form of an animal, visible only to those to whom it wishes to be visible. The rest of the world wonders about Elwood P. Dowd and his alleged invisible rabbit, Harvey. Elwood's aunt, Veta Louise Simmons, weary of being shunned from social circles, enlists the help of Judge Omar Gaffney to declare Elwood incompetent and commit him to Chumley's Rest. Elwood is happy to go if it makes Veta Louise happy. However, Dr. Willie Chumley, chief psychiatrist and owner of the rest home, not only sees Harvey but adores him as much as Elwood, even proposing to go to Cleveland with Harvey. Realizing that Elwood P. Dowd is perhaps the healthiest and sanest among them, Dr. Chumley reveals Veta Louise's vicious plot, including her seizures of Elwood's assets, and asks, "Good heavens, man, have you no righteous indignation?" Elwood explains his inspirational philosophy of life: "My mother always used to say to me, 'Elwood . . . she always called me Elwood . . . In this life, you can be oh so smart or oh so pleasant. I tried smart. I prefer pleasant. You may quote me.'"

Therein lies the inspiration for this tale of, shhhhhh!!!, ethics. Conventional wisdom holds that in business, you can be oh so smart, or you can be oh so ethical. Actually, the two are not mutually exclusive. You can be smart, ethical, and successful. In fact, get rid of ethical and success will elude you, or be fleeting at best. And so the tale of Edgar and Ari.

Edgar and Ari
Honesty Is a Tough Thing

It was 7:05 A.M. Pacific Time when Edgar P. Benchley arrived at his desk at Tortoise Enterprises and did what he always did at 7:05 A.M. Pacific Time every workday of the year: He sighed. The sigh filled his chest and heaved his shoulders as it brought his arms to rest on a desk filled with the paper trail of the troubles of the world—or at least the troubles of Tortoise Enterprises.

It wasn't that Edgar hated work, his desk, or even Tortoise Enterprises. Edgar was a born salesman, a whiz with numbers, and a master at SWOT analysis—the old strengths, weaknesses, opportunities, and threats. In fact, Edgar owned Tortoise Enterprises, a respectable company with respectable earnings, respectable products, respectable employees, respectable suppliers, respectable ads, and an asbestos-free building.

But Edgar's sigh was because of all that respectability—the lack of asbestos he could live with. Edgar was cursed with respectability and sighs. The rest of the world didn't always value respectability. How well Edgar had learned this lesson.

What made Edgar sigh, respectable, and asbestos-free was a secret Edgar had kept for a lifetime. Edgar had a pooka. Pookas are mythical creatures not everyone can see. They latch onto those they like and these poor souls not only see their pookas, they also begin living their lives to please them. But Edgar didn't have the kind of fun-loving, imbibing pooka that Jimmy Stewart was blessed with in the movie *Harvey*. Jimmy and his 6' 3" white rabbit pooka spent a great deal of time in bars. Edgar could have lived his life as a lush, sigh free.

Instead, Edgar was blessed with a different kind of rabbit pooka (though a tall one at that), who read Aristotle, quoted Thoreau, was well versed in Kohlberg's scale of moral development, and never had a good word to say about plaintiffs' accident lawyers. Edgar's pooka, nicknamed "Ari," was a rabbit that loved respectability, honor, and checks that truly were in the mail.

Ari had been a thorn in Edgar's side and a sigh in his chest for as long as Edgar could remember. His first vivid memory of seeing Ari was in the back seat of a forest green Dodge Polara being piloted by his lead-foot mother who was forever—as long as Edgar could remember, even before he remembered Ari—late. In fact, when Edgar first saw Ari in the back seat that day he assumed it was something out of *Alice in Wonderland* and the rabbit would simply chastise his mother for always being late, late for very important dates. However, Ari was not there to chastise Mrs. Vera Benchley for her tardiness. Ari had a much bigger "agenda," as many would come to use the term in Edgar's later years.

Ari appeared for the first time just after Edgar's mother, while speeding, cut through a corner shopping plaza to avoid stopping for a red light. From the back seat, Edgar asked his mom, "Isn't that illegal, Mom, and aren't you speeding?" Edgar's mother responded, "Yes, but we'll be on time for church." Edgar hadn't learned management lingo at the ripe old age of eight but his thoughts were along the line of the deliverables somehow being inconsistent with the mission and values statements. And as Edgar was sorting through his thoughts, which in his eight-year-old mind took the form of, "I wonder if the other mothers speed on their way to church," he turned to his left and saw the tallest rabbit in the world sitting next to him. Actually, it was the tallest anything Edgar had ever seen, with the exception perhaps of the Paul Bunyon statue the Benchleys had stopped to see near Brainerd, Minnesota, while they were traveling to see Edgar's uncle who had a woodchipping business in Fargo, North Dakota.

Not only was the rabbit tall, it was shaking its head. Edgar's still-vivid fear from that day was that he would be carried away in the claws of this creature (for surely rabbits this large had claws), to its hutch where he would become a sacrifice for his mother's speeding and avoidance of traffic signals, a civil misdemeanor in Edgar's community, but apparently a far greater offense in the kingdom of large animals. And Edgar's mother had read enough Beatrix Potter to him for him to realize that he would face the perils of Jemima Puddle-Duck, watering cans, Mr. McGregor's garden and hoe, and sly and not-so-sly foxes in the fairy tale world of rabbits (well, at least those in Great Britain).

Edgar tried to vocalize the claws theory and his accompanying fear to his mother, but Mrs. Vera Benchley was otherwise occupied, passing, cutting off other drivers, and offering hand gestures as she sped merrily along to church. Edgar tried to avoid eye contact with the gigantic creature because he had another theory that fire would dart from its eyes and singe his hair as well as his tweed wool slacks, thus turning his mother's hand gestures toward him. "Never mind that huge rabbit's eyes, look what you've done to the pants I just got out of layaway at the Bon-Ton!" would be his mother's sympathetic reaction. But as he peeled his eyes ever forward, Edward noticed that the rabbit's ears, the size of loaves of French bread, were clearly visible in the Polara's rear-view mirror. Ha! It was just a matter of time until Vera spotted those giant ears, pulled over, and beat this creature senseless with her patent leather purse, not so much for being an odd creature in her car but for costing her the extra time she had purchased with so many traffic violations.

But Vera, as Edgar referred to his mother—but only in the quiet recesses of his mind and the Polara's back seat—never saw the ears that Ray Charles would have sensed were present. And there would be no physical chastisement of this mutant rabbit by Mrs. Vera Benchley. Rather, Edgar, eyes wide open and facing front, began receiving a pummeling at the hands, er, feet of this creature. Edgar tried to move, hoping that the rabbit simply wanted to stretch out in their spacious and gracious Polara, but as he edged to the right of the car, so did the rabbit and those feet! When Edgar was clanking against the metal door handle of the sturdy Polara, Vera finally exclaimed: "Get away from the door handle. You'll fly out when I turn the corner." (Seat belts were not an issue in Edgar's youth, for Mrs. Vera Benchley held firm to the belief that all cars were safe at any speed. There being no mandatory buckle-up laws in those days, children often flew gleefully about the wide open spaces of sedans with pointed tail fins. Further, even if she had been converted to product liability, Mrs. Benchley was not the type to expend precious moments on added tasks in the form of phrases such as, "Buckle up, Edgar!") It was not what Edgar was expecting—his mother made no reference to the rabbit. Edgar swore his mother had X-ray vision enabling her to see through his bedroom door and to accompany him to school and back, for she knew everything he had done wrong before he even realized it was wrong. Yet, Vera Benchley did not see the rabbit feet the length of a Red Flyer wagon handle pushing Edgar against the door handle.

Edgar was weighing his choices: flying out the door of a Dodge Polara at 60 mph in a 40-mph zone or taking up residence with giant rabbits in a hutch that would surely be the size of the A&P. Both options seemed to involve broken bones, so Edgar made eye contact with the creature. The creature halted the pummeling temporarily and spoke, "Ari here. Short for Aristotle. Trying to help out your mother a bit. She is one reckless driver. You should tell her." Edgar was shaking in his Buster Browns but felt compelled to defend Mrs. Vera Benchley, "She doesn't get tickets. She's just trying to be on time." Ari's feet were positioned for further attack when Edgar asked, "Since when are kids in charge of parents?" Ari's response was simple, "When the parents won't see me but need some help, that's when I recruit the kids. And you, kid, you have to learn to speak up on these things. Think about this—your mother wants to get to church on time so she drives like a bat out of hell." Edgar interrupted, "We don't say 'hell' in our house." Ari continued, "Maybe not, but your mother drives like a demon. It's not right. Speak up!" Edgar hesitated, but Ari's feet were poised, so he sighed and blurted out, "Mom, maybe we should slow down." Mrs. Vera Benchley responded gleefully, "Ha! We're here with forty-two seconds to spare. Next time we'll slow down."

Each Sunday after that fateful encounter with that beast of the back seat, Edgar arose very early, readied himself in his go-to-meeting clothes and nudged his mother along in her preparations so that they always left the house for church with more than forty-two seconds to spare even in full compliance with the traffic code and general driver decorum. Edgar was determined to keep the rabbit out of the Polara. But Edgar would soon learn that once Ari entered your life, he didn't vanish quite as quickly as he appeared.

Ari was always around when Mrs. Vera Benchley embarked upon treacherous territory. Yet he never appeared to Mrs. Vera Benchley;

Ari was visible only to Edgar and he pummeled away until Edgar saw things Ari's way. In Ari's rabbit mind, there was no other way to see things except his way. There was the time in the grocery store parking lot when Mrs. Vera Benchley discovered, after loading all the groceries into the Polara, a box of Tide detergent on the bottom of her grocery cart. She nearly forgot to load it into the car but she clearly knew she had forgotten to pay for it. Nonetheless, she tossed it into the Polara's grand trunk and muttered, "Looks like my lucky day." Edgar felt a strange twinge, but nothing more than a fleeting one. If you knew Mrs. Vera Benchley you knew that she made many people twinge for many reasons, her driving being only a starting point for twinge discussion.

So Edgar let the twinge pass, but when he tried to climb into the back seat of the Polara, he found himself sitting squarely on two large white feet, more like snowshoes, that proceeded to work their irritation. "Take the Tide back in and pay. Wouldn't be honest. Wouldn't be right," said the rabbit, boasting a tie-dyed t-shirt this fine grocery-shopping day. Edgar was never quite sure where and how Ari got his wardrobe, but he was not yet confident enough about this large woodland creature to ask.

When Mrs. Vera Benchley saw her son flailing about in the back seat and, of course, could not see the cause of such flailing, she threatened doctor's visits and medication while brandishing a finger of warning about hyperactivity. Edgar's flailing continued because he was saying, "No!" as Ari was saying, nearly breathless from the serious pummeling, "Wouldn't be honest. Wouldn't be right." Edgar sighed, relented, and emerged from the car in one smooth gymnast's move, foisted by springy Ari feet, and urged his mother, "Mom, we have to pay for the Tide. Let's take it back in." Mrs. Vera Benchley resisted initially but then thought that perhaps the flailing was not hyperactivity but rather the result of Edgar's distress over swiping a five-pound box of Tide. She saw paying for the Tide as but a small fee to pay for silence in the car on the way home. Mrs. Vera Benchley and Edgar tromped back into the store with the Tide as Ari watched proudly from the back seat of the car. Edgar glanced back and thought that Ari was a pest, but a pleasant pest, the kind who seemed to know that what he wanted you to do would make you feel good.

The manager of the A&P could not gush over Mrs. Vera Benchley enough. Her honesty, her integrity, her trouble, her time—the manager with an apron and a load of pomade on his hair thought so much of Mrs. Vera Benchley that he gave Edgar a Zagnut candy bar. Edgar didn't like Zagnuts and, truth be told, the Zagnut was a bit stale, but Edgar had been taught by Mrs. Vera Benchley to thank those who offered him treats even in circumstances when the treats were as repulsive as Zagnuts—stale ones at that. Mrs. Vera Benchley's penchant for fudging a bit here and there also permitted her the graciousness of the white lie. As far as Edgar knew, Mrs. Vera Benchley was the only person in town who could convincingly tell the mayor's wife, who tipped the scales at 260 pounds, that she looked thinner. And Mrs. Vera Benchley could convince Eulalie McKechnie Pomeroy that she was *Vogue* material whenever Mrs. Pomeroy put on a new outfit. Edgar loved watching his mother in action on those occasions, but Ari stood by during the Pomeroy/Benchley encounters, large rabbit foot tapping, annoyed that he was powerless over Mrs. Vera Benchley and even more annoyed that Edgar enjoyed watching Mrs. Vera Benchley bending the truth. In those early years, Ari chose his battles with Edgar carefully. Ari's philosophy was to start with speeding and Tide and work his way up to the issues of transparently false flattery. Ari placed great faith in Kohlberg's scale of moral development and had great hopes for Edgar's progression.

Edgar left the grocery store wondering whether the Zagnut treat was perhaps something the pomade manager didn't want anyway.

Edgar's suspicions were confirmed when he returned to the car, proudly displaying his not-so-desirable reward to Ari. Ari, who seemed very knowledgeable about complex subjects Edgar had never heard of, such as depreciation, explained, "It was part of an inventory write-down anyway. But, it's the thought that counts." Edgar was beginning to enjoy Ari during these moments when Ari waxed philosophical or expounded on life, or, in this case, revenue offsets for grocers. Edgar was learning that Ari was not a man, er, rabbit of many words, but when he spoke he had something worth-while to say.

But there were those occasions when Ari was terribly rigid. There was that time in fifth grade when Mrs. Vera Benchley gave Edgar a truly awful haircut and Ari became most unreasonable. Edgar had asked for a buzz, just like the other guys. Mrs. Vera Benchley was blessed abundantly with creativity in both bending the truth and in home activities. She took to home barbering— having trained suffi-ciently, she thought, on the family terrier. However, dog hair and human hair do have their differences, in everything from texture to length, so Mrs. Vera Benchley was thrown for a loop when Edgar's hair proved easier plowing than Jack's, the friendly terrier who now had the distinct look of a Chihuahua. Mrs. Vera Benchley did man-age to buzz Edgar's hair, but not without several nicks to the head that gave Edgar something of a Dalmatian look. Edgar was embar-rassed and begged not to go to school the next day. As Ari listened intently from the arched doorway in the kitchen, Edgar's mother suggested, "Just put a Band-Aid over the big nick and tell them you fell while climbing in a cave. The excitement of a cave adventure will detract from the smaller nicks. You could even throw in a story or two about bats and snakes." Edgar was a born salesman, largely because of his mother's inherent abilities. He tried the art of persua-sion, but Mrs. Benchley had already moved on to cleaning up the hair from Edgar's, ahem, trim, even as Jack the terrier cowered in the corner terribly fearful and in a daze over his newfound diversity of species.

That Mrs. Vera Benchley had her moments. Missing school was not an option for Edgar, but at least she had found a way to cover the hair debacle for him. Edgar knew his mother was unique. Edgar's father, Mr. Wallace Benchley, said so nearly every day: "They threw out the mold after they made your mother, son. Perhaps it's just as well, too." Mr. Wallace Benchley was a deferential soul who followed the guidance and direction of Mrs. Vera Benchley mostly because he believed it to be an exercise in futility to think that he could change his flamboyant spouse. He had, however, drawn the line with her home barbering once he caught a glimpse of Edgar's buzz. In fact, so relieved was he that it was Edgar and Jack who had been the guinea pigs in the home barbering experiment that Wally Benchley approved of the spelunking story, Band-Aids and all. With this much parental guidance and consent, and missing school not an option, Edgar left for his room to prepare the yarns he would spin about stalactites and stalagmites for his classmates the next day as he recounted his cave derring-do and injuries at the hands of flying vermin. His mother was in some ways a genius, thought Edgar.

Until Ari appeared.

Ari had been distracted during the Wally, Vera, and Edgar hair-and-school debate by a rerun of "Sky King." Ari could debate moral relativism with the best of them, but he had a weakness for the tales of airplane rescues on the Flying Crowne Ranch. "I listened to "Sky King" on the radio before TV got hold of it," he often told Edgar.

But, with the latest close call now resolved by the single-engine Cessna and Penny *et al.*, Ari now stood in Edgar's room and shook his paw or leg or whatever one calls the appendages of large mythical animals. "Wouldn't be honest, Edgar. Wouldn't be right," he said.

"Really, Ari," Edgar argued, "I understand the speeding, the laundry detergent, and all those times you made my mother put back the tip she found left on the table when we went to restaurants. You were talking about someone else's money. And with my mother's driving you were worried about a four-car pileup, maybe five. But, this little tale about my hair hurts no one. It's the Eulalie McKechnie Pomeroy thing that I've seen you let pass. A little white lie. I'm saved humiliation. In fact, I'll be a hero. Besides, why is it their business that money is tight around here, thanks to you making us give back tips and pay for everything at the grocery store."

Ari's arms were crossed as he listened to Edgar's tale of woe and then asked, "Where was the cave?" Edgar paused, "I don't know where any caves are!" Ari was poised to pummel when Edgar saw the giant rabbit's wisdom. Edgar sighed. One question about specifics on the caveman story and he was toast. Ari had already begun playing with Edgar's toy anatomical man, fascinated with the spleen and its ease of removal as he distractedly mumbled, "Wouldn't be honest. Wouldn't be right."

So, Edgar went to school with nicks in full view, and Ari by his side, not in view to anyone, smiling proudly. "Doesn't it feel great not to hide anything?" Ari asked. Edgar sighed and assured Ari, "No, I feel like an idiot. I look like an idiot. And if I wasn't afraid of being called crazy more than being seen with these nicks and this hair, or the lack thereof, I'd tell everyone about you. They might get you for child abuse." In an elementary schoolyard where wearing last year's tennis shoes is grounds for a merciless taunting—it was quite easy for an invisible rabbit to feel confident but for Edgar, the resulting fashion disrepute would carry well into the sophomore year of high school. Who knew how harsh the penalty would be for haircuts that are an affront to society in the prime grade school years?

When Edgar arrived in class, there was a mighty starefest all around. The boys howled and the girls giggled over the no-pattern baldness that had consumed Edgar's head. Ari was in the back of the classroom appearing to be fascinated by sentence diagrams, muttering comments about "good," "well," "adverbs," and "adjectives." Miss Hazel Wertz, Edgar's fifth grade teacher, watched as Edgar endured the teasing. Miss Hazel Wertz was fully familiar with the colorful Mrs. Vera Benchley and knew that Edgar's lot in life was not easy, so she'd developed a soft spot in her heart for Edgar. Just when Edgar thought he could not stand it any longer and was tempted to try the cave story sans Band-Aid, Miss Wertz piped up, "You never know. Edgar's hairstyle might be ahead of its time." Miss Wertz's remark would puzzle Edgar for a lifetime. How could she have known that creative buzz cuts with words, symbols, and profanity etched into heads would be cool one day? The Wertz intervention ended the taunting.

While Edgar had hung his head during the Wertz remarks, afraid of any eye contact with his callous classmates, he did manage to lift his head and eyes slightly to the right when Miss Wertz closed her case on the nouveau hair theory. There, looking right at him, was Elise McDonough. The scuttlebutt of the schoolyard was that Elise was the most beautiful girl, not just in Franklin Elementary, but in the tri-county area. Edgar had to raise his eyes twice again because he thought that Elise was smiling at him, something that could not possibly happen to Edgar Benchley—especially Edgar Benchley with a caveman haircut. But, each time Edgar's eyes wandered over to the right and caught the elegant Elise, he saw the same smile. Edgar shared his thoughts on the Elise moment with Ari, "I thought she was smiling at me, you know, a friendly smile. But, she's Elise McDonough, and I'm, well, Edgar Benchley. She must have been laughing at me." Ari smiled as Edgar reminisced about his Elise moment.

Ari continued to be a tiresome stickler about honesty. And sometimes he didn't pummel, he just moped. Edgar wasn't sure which he minded more, because a disappointed large white rabbit sitting around crestfallen is tough to ignore. If Edgar answered the phone and it was for his mother, but his mother said, "Tell them I'm not here," Ari was there with a "Tsk, tsk!" and yet another "Tsk!" If Edgar appeared ready to tell the caller his mother was not there, Ari would mumble, "Wouldn't be honest. Wouldn't be right." Edgar, understanding how absolutely awful it was to have a large white rabbit moping around and muttering about lost values and commandments and all manner of integrity, would say into the phone, "Yes, here she is!" Edgar would sigh as his mother grabbed the phone and gave him a look that would freeze Popsicles in the Mojave in July. Edgar got into more hot water than lobsters in Maine when he listened to Ari. But Edgar preferred the punishment his mother would dole out for being a wiseacre over the emotional distress of a disappointed Ari.

Ari Goes to High School and Meets the Gang

Playing by the Rules Means Living with an Occasional Setback

A ri loved school and rarely missed a day. On those occasions when Edgar was ill, Ari would still attend and provide Edgar with the day's details, right down to what was served for lunch in the school cafeteria, as well as a report on the lovely Elise McDonough. Edgar had spent all of his school years turning his eyes and head as inconspicuously as he could for a look at Elise. Ari was as charmed by Elise as Edgar but for very different reasons. Ari used the term "impeccable character" in describing Elise while Edgar used the lingo of the day, "She's a fox, Ari!" Edgar still stood by his notion that Elise had smiled at him that long, lonely, and awkward haircut day in fifth grade.

Ari also paid attention at school, not so much to the teachers, but to the plans Edgar and his friends made to avoid the work that necessarily accompanies the difficult task of learning. Particularly annoying to Edgar's friends was studying for tests.

19

In Advanced Placement History, the American Revolutionary War was challenging for Edgar and his friends because there were far too many battles, generals, and twists and turns between victory and defeat, and their teacher, Mr. Omar Gallinger, gave demanding assignments. So, Drew Peters, Edgar's closest friend since first grade, hatched a plan in the cafeteria to conquer the rigorous exams of AP History.

Drew entered the cafeteria with Steve Thomas and Heather Gardiner. Initially they had decided that they would work together, develop an outline, and then study their heads off so they would know Cornwallis from Gates. But when they realized how many Gates, dates, and British mates were involved in the Revolutionary War, they decided to skip the middleman, that is, the brain, and write the information on their wrists and palms for the exam.

Upon hearing this, Ari, who had heretofore been bemoaning the low-fat tacos served in public school cafeterias, suddenly had his ears standing straight toward the ceiling, making him taller than Wilt Chamberlain. Edgar received a rabbit foot to the ribs and the warning "Wouldn't be honest. Wouldn't be right." Edgar no longer tried to reason with Ari in public because he had discovered, during the shaved-head incident in fifth grade, that the penalty for reasoning with air was about five years of ostracism. And in those pre–cell phone days, conducting such monologues was not the clearest path to acceptance in mainstream high school circles. So, Edgar never spoke to Ari in public. There were the knowing looks and the raised eyebrows (on Edgar's part), but no conversations, especially not in the cafeteria. Edgar remained silent. Drew, Steve, and Heather were already discussing whether permanent ink Sharpies or Vis-à-Vis pens would work best for the wrists and palms, or perhaps a combination of both.

Ari was now leaning back on the cafeteria bench with his back feet poised to pummel Edgar. But Edgar remained ever silent and those rabbit feet went like Thumper's against Edgar's hip, arm, and upper thigh, and he sighed deeply to avoid detection from the motion of invisible rabbit feet pounding on him like the drum solo from "In-A-Gadda-Da-Vida." And with that sigh, Edgar blurted out, "Isn't this cheating?" Ari turned and put his feet back to the ground and smiled. Drew looked mildly startled, but then regrouped. (Edgar was, after all, the son of Mrs. Vera Benchley, so those in the town had come to expect a certain level of bluntness from the Benchleys, the one exception to this social norm being the portly Mrs. Eulalie McKechnie Pomeroy who knew the Benchleys only for their gracious ways.)

"No," Drew assured. "These are not answers. They're just memory pegs."

Edgar almost forgot himself and turned to look smugly at Ari who he was sure would now understand that this was in fact a good and decent plan. But when he turned he saw those feet coming his way. Edgar blurted out, "Well, if it's not a problem then let's go and ask Mr. Gallinger if we can do it."

Omar Gallinger hadn't smiled once in the twenty-five years he had taught American history and was to most students what the troll was to the Billy Goats Gruff. Why, on Halloween, small children ran past his house. No one was sure whether they feared Omar Gallinger himself or that he might be handing out a summary of the Battle at Bunker Hill as a treat.

Drew, Steve, and Heather looked at Edgar as if he did indeed have a large and philosophical rabbit sitting next to him. They were stunned, and Edgar wasn't sure if it was because of the proposed revelation of the scam or simply at the notion of talking one-on-one with Gallinger. Nonetheless, they knew that the Benchley in Edgar would give him enough chutzpah to approach Omar the troll. But *they* had no intention of risking life, limb, or grade by speaking to Gallinger, so Steve simply responded to Edgar, "Are you in or out?"

Ari's face came around in front of Edgar, with those two big teeth smiling at him and a paw pointed to his feet. Ari employed pummeling in desperate times, but he could be charming and whimsical when he knew Edgar was coming around to his view on a proposed course of conduct. Edgar sighed and said, "I'm out."

Edgar and Ari left the cafeteria, although no one noticed Ari leaving, despite his rather heated soliloquy on the quality of public school lunches. Drew, Steve, and Heather watched sadly as their friend Edgar left. "He'll be studying all weekend. And what for?" Drew said. "Sometimes he's such a schmuck." Edgar hadn't noticed, but Elise McDonough, standing next to Drew, had a sad but oddly sympathetic look in her eyes. The elegant Elise was the most popular girl in school and Drew was her steady. Ari had expressed his disapproval of Elise's choices in boyfriends, but was still willing to attest to her impeccable character. Edgar's crestfallen state that day of the declined memory pegs would not allow him to lift his eyes from the speckled linoleum of the cafeteria to see what Ari later explained to Edgar was Elsie's "look of admiration."

Edgar's shoulders even drooped as he left school that day. The prospect of spending the full weekend with General Cornwallis and the Green Mountain Boys had sunk in. He now regretted having run past Mr. Gallinger's house all those Halloweens during grade school because if the rumors were true, he might have collected the complete set of Gallinger study guides for American history.

Edgar was down, but he didn't feel like a schmuck, not around Ari. He never felt like a schmuck with Ari around because Ari brought a feeling Edgar had come to know well since the time Ari first set paw in the back seat of the Polara. It was the feeling, still so vivid, he first felt that day in the parking lot when he and his mom returned to the grocery store to pay for the Tide. Ari had sparked in Edgar a boldness that was enormously gratifying. And so as Edgar left school he looked up at Ari and once again was lifted by that old feeling that first came to him with that Zagnut he earned in exchange for a paid-for box of Tide.

On Monday morning, Drew, Heather, Steve, and Edgar all arrived on time for Mr. Gallinger's test. Ari was a tad late—he had tarried to witness Edgar's mother claiming to the optical company that a pair of glasses she had broken when she sat on them were so defective that they had imploded and that she needed a new pair under her warranty. All Ari could do was click his mythical rabbit tongue, as he had no influence over Mrs. Benchley. Ari often used Edgar to rein Vera in, but Ari had weighed carefully the lesser of the evils this morning (he had taught Edgar this principle on resolving dilemmas involving conflicting values long ago). Ari hated truancy and tardiness, especially on test days, and choosing between the two simultaneous dilemmas, he was forced to endure Mrs. Benchley's optical deception because Edgar's schedule conflict prevented his intervention to help Mrs. Benchley see the issue, as it were, more clearly. Ari did, however, make a note to have a discussion on nature versus nurture with Edgar, the presently inaccessible offspring of the ethically challenged Mrs. Benchley. Drew, Heather, and Steve had most of the Revolutionary War outlined on their wrists, including a misspelling of Paul Revere and the numbers wrong in "one if by land and two if by sea." Edgar struggled with the exam as Ari sat nearby. While Ari was well known in the world of pookas for his knowledge in American history, he was of no help to Edgar. Ari helped only on questions of honesty, not on questions about turning points in wars. Instead, Ari sat and studied Mr. Gallinger's spectacular world map, which covered one whole wall of the classroom. Edgar struggled mightily with the details of the test, while Ari, out of respect for Edgar's concentration, spoke only occasionally to share thoughts such as, "When did West Pakistan become Bangladesh?"

In complete violation of the Family Educational Rights and Privacy Act, as Ari pointed out but did not fuss over, the students of Mr. Gallinger's AP History class exchanged test papers and graded each others' papers that very day in class. Drew, Heather, and Steve all earned A's on their exams. And Mr. Gallinger was none the wiser about the memory peg system. Edgar, on the other hand, earned only a B and a pat on the back with a rabbit paw. Edgar sighed and looked Ari squarely in the eyes. Edgar was irritated with Ari and there was no warm feeling about rabbits, right or wrong.

Not only had he not done as well on the exam, he had driven a bit of a wedge between himself and his friends. Edgar would have to work to get back in their good graces. Right now he was only in the good graces of a mythical and invisible rabbit, and Edgar was feeling the pain from his choice of rabbit over man. Edgar asked Ari, "If I did the right thing, how come they didn't get caught and got higher grades? And if I did the right thing, how come I'm the one who's not popular?"

Ari leaned back on his haunches and gave a contemplative look he saved for when Edgar doubted his wisdom. There was always a pause as Edgar waited anxiously, and Ari knew he was thinking in true Benchley fashion, although to himself, "When is this thing going to say and do something that's helpful and doesn't get me into trouble? What other human being has to cope with the curse of a philosophical rabbit with higher standards than my parents?" But Ari said what he always said, "Wouldn't be honest. Wouldn't be right," but then added, "Wait, my boy, you'll see. The race isn't over yet." Then Ari instructed, "Besides, Edgar, look up and to your right." There was Elise McDonough smiling at Edgar. And this time Edgar witnessed the smile, which was clearly not one of derogation.

Ari and the Reunited Fab Four at College

Doing the Right Thing Often Means More Work

By the time of their senior year in high school, Edgar, Drew, Heather, and Steve had let history test bygones be bygones. They had made peace with each other, for the memories of Drew, Heather, and Steve were truly quite short in all aspects of life, not just history. Drew, Heather, and Steve continued to rely on the memory peg system and Edgar and Ari relied on just memory. They coexisted, the American history wedge dissipated, and Ari did not demand that Edgar abandon his ethically edgy pals. They were, once again, the Fab Four, ready to conquer the world, or at least see what the world outside the town limits looked like.

Drew, Heather, and Steve, thanks largely to their fine performances in their AP classes and the memory peg system, all managed to earn scholarships to State University. Edgar also secured admission to State University but with a lesser scholarship because his studying had not yielded the grades of Drew, Heather, and Steve. Edgar would have to work part time to go to State, and secured a job at a tollbooth on the expressway. Ari loved their job because he enjoyed predicting which cars would attempt to drive through without paying. Ari was eventually reduced to vehicle profiling, as the Carerra, Mercedes, and Jaguar drivers seemed far more likely to be drive-throughs than, say, your drivers of Buicks and wagons of all species.

The four (only Edgar knew that there was an invisible fifth) moved onward and upward together. Edgar had pointed out to Ari, though, that despite their flagrant cheating in high school, Drew, Heather, and Steve all got to the same place—State University. And they did so with better scholarships. Worse, Edgar continued, he had spent weekends studying, while Heather became homecoming queen; Drew was voted "Most Likely to Succeed"; and Steve was salutatorian. Ari just raised an eye whisker, which was Edgar's signal to be silent. If Edgar continued whining about his friends' successes and achievements well beyond Edgar's humble benchmarks (and there was a term Ari had taught him in their many discussions of new management trends), Ari just made his usual comments: "Wouldn't be honest. Wouldn't be right," "Wait, kid, you'll see," and finally, "The race isn't over yet."

The four all majored in business at State University, and prepared for careers as what Drew described as "moguls." Edgar wasn't sure that Drew even knew what the word meant. The Benchley in Edgar often wanted to tell Drew that he was not the sharpest tool in the shed, but since moving away from home and the influences of Mrs. Vera Benchley, Edgar had come to contain his bolder opinions. Ari had exercised some influence also. When Edgar bemoaned Drew's successes despite his lunkheadedness, Ari waxed philosophical. Drew never studied, Ari reminded Edgar. It wouldn't be a fair fight for Edgar to assume Benchley posture and explain to Drew exactly what his limits were. Edgar never told Ari so, but he loved the rabbit's restraint. Oh, Ari was merciless when he was molding and shaping Edgar, and the pummelings were brutal and often difficult to conceal. But there was a calmness in Ari's detached view and an odd compassion for others despite his brutality toward Edgar.

The three apprentice moguls were preoccupied with social life and continued with their aversion to cracking books. The state of grade inflation being what it was, they simply crammed a few Organizational Behavior terms such as "human capital" and "emotional intelligence" into their heads before exams, and proceeded to make the dean's list. Edgar, on the other hand, was attending school with a rab bit of high standards. Ari had read every book Peter Drucker had written and predicted the writing of *If Aristotle Ran General Motors.* Ari said he would run things differently and one day someone would write about his thoughts on GM. Ari also knew Friedman and Becker economics and demanded that Edgar do no less. New business guru Ken Blanchard got much more than a minute of discussion time as Edgar and Ari together explored the nuances of business success and failure along with the proper booking of executive options and the propriety of taking capital expenses from ordinary income.

The one bothersome part of college for Edgar's friends was the ubiquitous term paper. Heather, Drew, and Steve had a smooth glide through the women's studies term paper. "Just be sure to write something about the oppressive male, the epidemic of sexual harassment, women in combat (you're for it, of course), and spousal abuse during the Super Bowl, and you've got an A in that course," was Steve's advice. Heather, Drew, and Steve developed grand papers for their women's studies course incorporating a good bashing of Barbie and a dose of Simone de Beauvoir.

Ari would not permit Edgar to "spout politically correct platitudes." Ari told Edgar that for the figures on Super Bowl abuse to be correct, hospital emergency rooms would have to be filled, and, as Ari explained, quite the opposite was true on Super Bowl Sunday. "Everyone is watching the game. Really, it's a calm Sunday after all." Ari was perhaps one of the few political pookas around. Edgar had asked Ari if a pooka with Ted Kennedy's views was available. Ari assured him it was not possible to combine his role with those views.

So, Edgar wrote a paper dispelling the feminine mystique. Most of the women from Edgar's women's studies course shunned him. But one day after class, two women came up to Edgar and said they admired his bold stance and had even been swayed by his arguments. Still Edgar's professor gave him a C on the paper, unheard of in a lower division college course.

"Who would have been hurt by a term paper that said what the professor wanted to hear?" he asked Ari. "Are all the pookas like you? Isn't there a fine line here? I'm not cheating. I'm just not following the old "to thine own self be true," and I'm only violating it on term papers!"

Edgar knew as the whining left his lips that Ari did not deal in nuances. Ari offered his usual thought, "Wouldn't be honest. Wouldn't be right." And, of course, he added yet again, "Some day you'll understand why, and remember, the race is not over yet."

At Heather's apartment one fine spring afternoon Edgar, Drew, and Heather were having lunch and discussing their Business Policy term papers, which were due soon. Steve came bounding into Heather's apartment. He had big news, "Remember Elise McDonough?" Both Edgar's and Ari's ears perked up, although the effect on Ari was much more noticeable, at least to those who can see pookas. Steve continued, "She's graduating from Swarthmore—valedictorian!" Drew understood the implications of such an achievement for any future he might have had with Elise. Edgar barely had a chance to digest the news when Steve launched into a new topic.

He began spouting addresses and phone numbers. Steve had found companies that sold term papers on all topics. "And," Steve added, "that free market stuff we aced in Econ applies. The A papers cost more than the C papers."

Edgar had been working swing and graveyard shifts at the toll-booth to support himself after his scholarship was reduced for receiving grades like the C in women's studies. Although he would have to work back-to-back shifts and double overtime, he was con-sidering purchasing the A paper. He leaned over Heather as she tele-phoned for information on the papers and Steve and Drew waited anxiously. To avert professorial attention from their scheme, they would choose different topics, different papers, and maybe even spruce them up a bit.

"Put in one typo and one misspelling for authenticity," counseled Drew. Edgar thought that if Drew's paper were to appear truly authentic, it should be filled with errors. Ari agreed— he seemed to have the ability to read Edgar's thoughts. (Also, Ari was not beyond the Benchley influence, gained apparently by nurture and not a gift by nature as from Mrs. Vera Benchley to Edgar.)

Ari, who was present in the apartment as the anxious phone calls were made to the term paper purveyors of fraud, had remained quiet, because he had been studying Heather's bagel cutter. Ari had long been fascinated by kitchen gadgets. Indeed, they distracted him and Edgar found himself hopeful that Heather's new garlic press would distract Ari sufficiently that the term paper deal could be closed before Ari had a chance to raise a whisker or a paw. However, deep into his cost-benefit analysis of the garlic press, Ari realized that Edgar was slipping once again. He strolled next to the phone in full view of Edgar and issued an "Ahem!" By this time—Ari had been with him for thirteen years—Edgar almost knew better than to argue. Edgar did issue a slight appeal with his eyes, communicating the lack of sleep that an additional paper would only exacerbate. Ari was not even preparing a pummel. In fact, he had moved on to a lava lamp in the corner. It wasn't a kitchen gadget, but there was something about a lamp that throws off heat and no light that intrigued the large curious rabbit.

While it seemed like a clean break, lava lamps being what they are and are not, Edgar had learned that despite Ari's lack of paws-on insistence, the discussion was over and the die was cast. Edgar had learned that when Ari has spoken and moved on to other things, it was best for Edgar to surrender. For some reason, though, Edgar didn't feel as if it were a surrender. Once again, Edgar felt that odd feeling of boldness and strength, that Ari had created in him so many years ago. Edgar didn't yet understand why this feeling came over him because, after all, Ari's decisions always meant more work, more trouble, more, more, more. But Edgar was coming to trust the feeling, so he turned away from his huddle of friends eagerly conspiring to abscond term papers, grabbed his backpack (a device that annoyed Ari, for he felt civilized humans used briefcases), and left. His friends remained behind, lava lamp boiling away, and their credit cards poised to purchase the expensive term papers.

Edgar worked around the clock to complete his term paper. He did not make it through the first draft without extensive murmuring and griping. As Ari explored the number of green M & Ms in a one-pound bag, Edgar fumed: "There is nothing in a paper entitled 'The Shifting Paradigms of TQM, Six Sigma, MBO, Incentive Pay, and 360-degree Feedback,' that is going to do me any good in life. I could have bought a term paper, no one would have known, and I wouldn't be wasting my time with this."

Ari responded with uncharacteristic input. "Frankly speaking," he said, "the topic lacks something." Even Ari could sense a breaking point. Ari chose his battles carefully. For example, despite his firm convictions about briefcases, he did not foist them upon Edgar and put up with what he called the "social humiliation" of a companion with a backpack. This management paper, and Edgar's rather Benchley-like critique, made for a clear breaking point. Ari knew when to fold them, although he found the game of poker inherently deceptive. So, in mid-sentence on his critique of Edgar's management paper draft, he stopped. This time Ari sensed the potential for flames from Edgar's eyes and simply offered his usual input and focused on his area of strength; after all, Ari had studied SWOT analysis as well. "But you can't buy term papers," he said, "Wouldn't be honest. Wouldn't be right. Someday you'll understand."

Drew, Steve, and Heather turned in their term papers, complete with spiral bindings, and earned A's. Of course, they had paid "A prices" for them from We Cheat, Inc. Edgar, on the other hand, earned a B for his efforts along with one comment from the professor: "The topic lacks something." Ari said nothing.

The Irony of the Job Hunt
Being Ethical Sometimes Means Running Behind in the Race

Edgar finished college with a respectable 3.5 GPA. Yet, Drew, Steve, and Heather had higher ones, well into those laude categories. In fact, Drew had five job offers from multinational corporations. He had accepted all five and was still interviewing. When Edgar suggested that Drew decide and maybe toss him the leftovers, Drew responded, "Everyone does this. Besides, if anything goes wrong at these companies, do you think for one minute they wouldn't cut me loose?" Ari was truly appalled at Drew's behavior and even considered allowing Edgar to make the speech he had kept inside for so long, in complete contravention to Benchley genetics.

Drew talked Steve and Heather into using the same approach. In the lucrative world of multiple offers and multiple acceptances, among the three of them, they had secured eighteen job offers. They accepted all of them and continued to interview, waiting and holding out for more and better, unbeknownst to those companies still recruiting them.

Edgar thought he might join in on the job offer festivities that were springing from a heck of a bull market, born of trickle-down economics. And there was Ari, standing in the corner of Edgar's humble studio apartment, arms crossed and head shaking "No." It was the same shake of the head from long ago in the back seat of the Polara. Ari's ears flopped when he shook his head, and Edgar was nearly tempted to ignore this unbecoming and anti-intellectual warning—it was unseemly to take career advice from such a preposterous beast. But being a mythical creature, Ari required no sleep and was not above keeping Edgar up at night until Edgar saw things Ari's way (which was, as Ari had long maintained, apparently the only way to see things). Further, Edgar hated the sleepless nights more than he hated the pummeling. So, Edgar went to his one and only interview and accepted a decent job offer. It wasn't an offer that compared with some of those of Drew, Steve, and Heather, and they were still going strong playing one company against another. But then Edgar's GPA wasn't what Drew's, Steve's, and Heather's were either.

Between the time that Edgar accepted the offer and graduation, the small company filed for Chapter 11 bankruptcy and instituted a hiring freeze. Edgar was now an unemployed college graduate who didn't speak to Ari for eight days. And he made no eye contact. In fact, Ari later confessed to some fear of Edgar's eyes containing lasers during this tense period of their relationship. Ari half-apologized: "Can I be held responsible for the poor management decisions in a company that could blow it in this economy?" And then he commented on the odds of failure in a bull market: "Someday you'll understand."

Edgar brooded for some time and was in a particularly foul mood when he and Ari were forced to take full-time employment at the tollbooth to meet their postgraduation expenses. But Ari, who had long enjoyed the profiling aspects of toll skippers, also reveled in the company of the humble souls who worked the tollbooths with Edgar. While some of them still talked of their fears of tollbooth work after seeing *The Godfather* and Sonny's untimely death at the Long Island Causeway tollbooth, they were for the most part a carefree and happy lot. Ari often listened intently to their discussions about coupons and this newfangled money-saving place called Sam's Club. Ari loved a thrifty soul, though not cheapskates, and a good bargain hunter was tops in Ari's book. Edgar wasn't quite as charmed as Ari with the discussions, coupons, or even *The Godfather*, but did allow in his private discussions with Ari that any tollbooth staffer beat Drew in brains and congeniality. As Edgar labored in the tollbooth, and Ari honed his auto profiling skills, the years passed with a few employment opportunities for Edgar that offered more money, but always less charm than state employment with the department of highways and byways.

The high point of Ari's and Edgar's public service career was when Elise McDonough came through their lane. Unless Edgar was mistaken, and Ari assured him he was not, Elise was warm, kind, and nonjudgmental when she spoke with Edgar. "The fumes must be making me hallucinate, Ari," explained Edgar about the Elise passthroughs, "Elise is out of my league, even just for a smile."

Elise had been hired at an investment banking firm, and Drew's information was that she had become "valedictorian" there as well. Edgar and Ari always knew Drew had vocabulary limits. Drew shared with Edgar the offense he had taken at Elise's utter rejection of his proposal of marriage. When Ari heard of Drew's unrequited love for the elegant Elise, he only muttered, "Impeccable character."

Drew Gets Edgar a Job

Expect a Little Mockery for Playing Ethically

Drew had kept himself rolling in offers until the ante was higher than even he had imagined. He went to work for Zenon, Inc., at a salary twice that of Edgar's long-gone job, four times that of Edgar's tollbooth wages, and in a position several layers up from Edgar's lonesome and now-defunct offer. Drew, since the days of high school, had always been one of those people who succeeded quickly. Within two years, he was made the head of a unit at Zenon.

Drew happened to drive through Edgar's bay at the toll station one morning. And he did so in style—in a brand-new royal blue Carerra. Ari looked nervous, and his apprehension didn't come from worrying that he might be run over by a Porsche. Ari was worried because he thought he had driven the tripartite of Drew, Steve, and Heather from Edgar's life, and now here was one of them returning in a high-speed auto.

Drew nearly passed through without recognizing Edgar, but when he saw him he couldn't resist the chance to taunt Edgar, a skill he first practiced in fifth grade and then used well through high school and college. So, he backed up the Carerra and said, "Edgar, you always were a schmuck. It's embarrassing to have an old friend working here. Look, here's my card. Call me. I'll get you a job."

Ari was even more nervous now, but he had no jurisdiction. Edgar going to work for a hotshot was no basis for a foot pummeling. Drew was offering Edgar a job at a company that had no pending indictments, no soft-money donations, and not even a *60 Minutes* camera crew hanging about the place.

With no resistance from Ari, Edgar called Drew—after he had finished his shift at the tollbooth, of course. Drew got Edgar a great job with a great salary in a company not in any trouble with the law and nowhere near Chapter 11 bankruptcy. When Edgar gave his supervisor at the tollbooth his notice, the supervisor, who seemed to be eighty-two years old if he was a day, said, "You'll be back." Edgar thought it was a mighty odd thing to say and not very flattering, but Ari seemed to like the old codger, so Edgar simply wished him well.

Because Edgar had earned a minor in accounting, Drew put him in charge of keeping the books for his unit. Both Edgar and Ari enjoyed the extra work space, now that they were out of the tollbooth (and the extra salary even found Edgar leaving his studio apartment behind, with Ari now enjoying his own bedroom), but Edgar was perplexed after just three months in his new digs.

"How can you sell parts in a warehouse that are worth $1 million for $11 million? And what kind of a company makes such a bad deal?" Edgar asked himself.

Ari generally passed the time with Space Invaders, a new game sensation that Drew had put in every office, as a capital expenditure, of course. However, one of Ari's ears always did perk up when he heard Edgar wonder aloud. Still, Edgar's accounting self-inquiries did not trouble Ari much. Even Ari understood (although Drew seemed clueless), that Edgar was a young man with only a minor in accounting. Hence only one of Ari's ears ever rose on the inquiry. Ari's ear raising was a half-hearted sort of indignation.

But as the days went by, Ari's Space Invaders concentration was broken with more questions from Edgar on accounting proprieties. "How do you report income from a contract for a sale that won't take place until 2010?" Edgar wondered aloud. "And shouldn't advertising be an expense taken from current income? How come we keep deferring all of these costs?"

Ari had stopped playing Space Invaders. And Edgar was talking to Ari and himself more with each passing day. Ari also noticed that Edgar's accounting self-inquiries were becoming more sophisticated. This young man was well past the simple concepts of debit here and credit there. Still, Ari didn't say much during Edgar's accounting epiphanies. But Edgar, who had been so resistant to Ari when it came to memory pegs, the purchase of papers, and job interviews, was a work in progress. Ari remained silent because his protégé was showing great promise all on his own. Ari was not yet comfortable enough to continue with Space Invaders, but he did not even need to resort to head-shaking, and he had not bothered Edgar once during sleep hours, something Edgar had explained to Ari were precious hours, sleep being a human necessity. Pookas are oblivious to time, body clocks, and wee hours.

"This inventory is worthless," Edgar said. "It needs to be written off. But, that's a heck of a hit for a quarter. That's a heck of a hit for the year." Even Ari was stunned at how much all that studying had paid off for Edgar. Edgar was doing auditors everywhere justice with his questions. But, Edgar also knew such a hit spelled financial trouble, which meant layoffs, which meant the old RIF (reduction-in-force) for those most recently hired, including himself, which meant back to the tollbooth-and-coupon discussions. Edgar saw the issue but wasn't inclined to rock the accounting boat with some squabbles over the timing of debits and credits.

As he saw his still-young charge waffling, Ari finally spoke up: "Edgar, I'm no accountant. Actually, I don't even use a CPA, but I am well versed in financial reporting, and it sounds like your books say, 'If it hadn't been for all of these expenses, we would have made money.' It isn't honest. It isn't right." Edgar sighed, but continued toiling away at his Drew-assigned tasks, saying nothing about the accounting issues. Ari knew Edgar was getting a bit old for the pummeling so he began employing more sophisticated tools of persuasion such as literary references, metaphors, drama in the form of pantomime, and even dribs and drabs of applicable songs. At one point during Edgar's accounting dilemmas, Ari was first humming and then singing, "That's the sound of the men working on the chain ga—eee—ang."

"I don't care, Ari. I'm not going back to the tollbooth. And you'll lose your bedroom! This is just accounting. There's room for interpretation. Remember my term paper on materiality and disclosure?"

Ari suddenly had another tune, "I fought the law and the law won. I fought the law and the law won."

Edgar was able to ignore Ari for three more weeks. He had just purchased a handsome dinette set with a hutch that Mrs. Vera Benchley deemed "perfect," and Edgar was not about to risk losing it to the finance company. Further, he had a down payment on a slightly used Corolla that would be his within two weeks. But Ari was diabolical on this one. He left *BusinessWeek* stories about Charles Keating, Michael Milken, and Crazy Eddie lying about the place with the numbers of years they were sentenced to highlighted along with their financial accounting theories. Three weeks into Ari's relentless campaign and two weeks before Edgar defaulted on his Corolla and dinette set, Edgar took his documents, findings, and limited accounting experience to Drew.

When Edgar explained his concern about the sale of the $1 million parts for $11 million, Drew had a simple response: "Edgar, this is a company with a billion dollars in revenue each year. It's called materiality. Not enough to worry about." Ari was not satisfied. Neither was Edgar, but he proceeded despite Drew's response.

When Edgar asked about the advertising expenses not being booked, Drew pointed to a formula showing that for every dollar spent on advertising, the company could expect income as the ads took hold about eighteen months later. "It only makes sense that we wait to book those expenses," Drew explained. Ari was getting agitated and his foot was tapping. His nose had been twitching for some time now.

By the time Edgar got to the worthless inventory issue, Drew had run out of accounting theory, explanations, and patience. "Look, Edgar. I got this job for you. Don't make trouble. Just do what I ask you to do and stop asking so many questions. Be a team player. For once, Edgar, be a team player. Don't you think there are people running this company with far more experience than you and I have? And how about the auditors? Do you think a firm with Arthur Andersen's reputation would sign off on something that wasn't right? They've been through here and have never said a word about any of the things you're worrying about."

Edgar glanced over at Ari with a "How about it?" look, but it was no use. Ari was preparing for a full Bruce Lee attack on Drew. Yes, Ari was so agitated by Drew and the lack of transparency in the unit's financials that he was prepared to resume pummeling, but this time of Drew. Of course, Drew could neither see nor hear Ari and he would never know or feel what hit him, but Ari assured Edgar that despite all those drawbacks he would feel better as a result of such an attack. Edgar had never seen Ari so openly hostile toward others, even Drew. Ari made Edgar uncomfortable at times and was generally a pest, but Edgar had never known Ari to resort to physical abuse of others, even if only in a mythological sense.

That night Edgar and Ari went to their respective bedrooms without a word or a twitch. Ari didn't even watch a video. He sat in his contemplative position. He was what the old IBM slogan of THINK had in mind. Ari was THINK, writ large, and in animal form. The silence in the apartment was that of no creature stirring. But by the next morning, the largest creature living there had indeed stirred. Ari was already in the nook when Edgar entered. There, in the breakfast nook, Edgar faced his pooka and the inevitable. (The pooka never missed starting his day with David Hartman and Joan Lunden. However, he was not crazy about Joan's shorter hair or recent weight gain.) Edgar broke the silence. "I can try to do something about this, or I can quit," he said. "Either way, I'm out of a job." Ari felt there was no need for his input; Edgar was headed in the right direction. Ari had belabored his points in the early days, but another of his more evolved, and now subtle and sophisticated new tactics was that of simple silence. The wrong direction, in Ari's mind, was staying at Zenon and doing absolutely nothing. But Ari and Edgar were also moving into that phase of the human and pooka relationship where the human does the bulk of the reflection without threat of force, especially from the force of the snowshoe-like feet of a very large rabbit.

"The problem is," Edgar said, "it seems like I can't get a break. And this business of honesty and right and wrong has done nothing but leave me in the dust. And here it is again. I'm back to the tollbooth while these guys cash in options for cooking the books. It isn't right."

"Well said," Ari noted, "It isn't right. But, it's not over. Someday you'll understand."

When Edgar went to work, he decided he would schedule an appointment with Drew's division head. Drew was Edgar's supervisor, but he was still relatively low in the management hierarchy. So Edgar booked an appointment with the division vice president. Armed with his charts, numbers, and FASBs, Edgar, with Ari in tow, told the division vice president that there were issues with contract pricing, booking revenues, and write-offs. The vice president listened intently then asked his assistant to hold all his calls. Edgar's hopes were up and his mind was racing. Oddly, Ari was already at the door, prepared to leave.

"Edgar, you're a bright lad, so I am only going to say this once. For your own good, stop behaving like Chicken Little. Do you have any idea what small potatoes you're talking about here in the grand scheme of business and in relation to this company's revenues? You guys with steel backbones drive me crazy. If we played by your rules, this country would look like Uzbekistan. We make quality products, we sell them, and we give investors a good return. You think we made up these rules? There's not a company in this industry, or any other for that matter, that isn't doing its books exactly the way we're doing ours. Now, this little discussion between you and me, it never happened. If you say you talked to me about this, I'll deny it. And, for your own good, Drew won't ever know you did this little end run. Can I count on you to be a team player?"

A sheepish Edgar, forgetting the rabbit waiting at the door, replied, "Yes."

Edgar gathered his papers, his GAAPs, his FASBs, and left. "The only thing that could make me more of a geek is a white pencil protector in my pocket," Edgar mumbled to himself as he approached Ari and the door. Ari's paws were crossed and one foot was lopped over the other as he watched Edgar's slow walk to the door. Ari took the time to respond to Edgar. "I heard that," he said. "And I agree with the white pencil deal completely."

But Ari agreed with Edgar's self-assessment for a different reason. "You shouldn't have said, 'Yes.' It isn't honest. It isn't right," he said. "Shoot higher." Edgar asked Ari exactly what he meant.

"Try the CEO," he replied.

Edgar thought CEO for the rest of the day and Ari chanted it that night so that Edgar spent yet another sleepless night. He finally confronted Ari at 2:00 A.M. "Why me?" he asked. "Why should I care when no one else does? And how come you always ask me to put my grades, my job, and my apartment on the line? How come everyone else gets ahead while I follow these rules about right and wrong that you impose on me in a world that doesn't care? Ari, if there were a drug for hyperactivity in ethics, I'd get you a prescription."

Ari smiled and continued his chanting: "C-E-O. C-E-O. C-E-O." When mentoring their charges, pookas are tireless. Ari chanted until 4 A.M.

Still, Edgar felt good about his life. It was that old, courageous pride that Ari had given to Edgar so many years before. It was a comfortable life, a life that had no secrets lurking like land mines about to explode, no regrets, and really, as Ari often pointed out, a solid knowledge base and some fine writing skills, with the exception of that one management paper. Edgar was surprised to find himself leaning toward doing what Ari wanted, not because Ari was pestering him, but because he realized that Ari might have a point. Perhaps a comfortable life has its own benefits, different from the fast lanes Drew, Steve, and Heather operated in.

So, at 4 A.M., Edgar got out of bed and penned a letter to the "C-E-O" outlining his concerns about the unit's books. He even attached exhibits to the letter, in a fabulously organized fashion—a skill he had picked up doing his paper on strategic management. He apologized for the intrusion of his letter, but pointed out that he had tried to follow the lines of authority. "The vice president," Edgar wrote, "suggested that I simply get back to work, but I felt this might be important to you and our company."

By 7:00 A.M., Edgar was done with his letter. Ari did the honors of tossing it in the mailbox on their way to the office. All that day and the next, Ari was back to Space Invaders.

Three days after mailing the letter, Edgar found a response waiting on his desk. He opened it and began reading. Oddly, Ari was once again by the door with his paws crossed. The letter read:

> *Dear Edgar:*
>
> *It is always good to have employees communicate directly with me. From such direct communication, I am able to discern the types of people we have working for us—whether they are a good fit, how hard they are working, whether they are team players, etc. Thank you for sharing your information with me. You are fired.*
>
> *Anyone who can't work with his supervisors and be a team player has no place in Zenon, Inc. We work together for the goals of quality, service, and returns. I regret that you are unable to commit to these values.*
>
> *Sincerely,*
> *Kevin Day, CEO*
> *Zenon, Inc.*

A security guard appeared shortly thereafter to oversee Edgar's packing up and to escort him from the building. Unbeknownst to the guard, he was escorting Ari out as well. Edgar knew he and Ari would be back in the cramped quarters again—the tollbooth and a studio apartment awaited. Edgar also gave Ari a piece of his mind as they packed to move. All those warm thoughts he had had about Ari before penning the letter to the CEO were gone. How on earth do you make spending just four months on your first real business job look good on a resume? "Ari," he said, "I can't keep doing this. My life is a shambles. I'm unemployed and I have a one-on-one relationship with a CEO who took the time to fire me personally. I wish I could understand why you are considered a good thing to have."

Ari, a pooka of great brevity, except when it came to political issues, responded, "Someday you'll understand."

CHAPTER 6

Heather Feels Sorry for Edgar and Gets Him a Job

Being Ethical Means You Have to Speak Up

Drew was no longer speaking to Edgar because he had taken tongue lashings from both the vice president and Kevin Day, CEO, for his role in bringing such an interloper into the company. However, Drew was still in touch with Heather and Steve. Drew shared the entire Edgar scenario with them, to which Steve responded, "He's such a geek." Heather, always the most charitable of the three, said, "He's a schmuck, but he's a likeable one. And at least he's consistent. Remember AP History and how he wouldn't use the memory pegs?"

Then Steve laughed and said, "How about that management paper he did instead of buying one? And he worked for seventy-two straight hours on it."

Heather announced, "But Edgar is a decent man. If I wanted something done and done right, I'd ask him. And if I needed help, he

47

would drop everything to come help me. He'd do the same for you, Steve. He's not like us—but that may not be such a bad thing. Don't you think all that he has done while we've been cutting corners gives him an air of nobility?"

Drew could not bring himself to agree, except to offer, "He's nothing like his mother. I like her." Steve was silent but had an odd sort of contemplative look, reminiscent of Ari's IBM looks. And then Steve added, "You know who really likes Edgar? Elise McDonough." Steve knew he had ruffled Drew's feathers or gills or whatever Drew had that were sensitive to offense. "I saw her the other day, and just like every other time I run into her, she asked me about Edgar. Says she respects him. Can you imagine? Girl like that making the money she does and she likes the dork in the toll-booth over you, Drew, the executive with the Porsche." There was a lengthy stretch of a wedge between Drew and Steve following these thoughts.

Heather concluded the three friends' periodic Edgar discussion, "I think I'll help Edgar out. He's been back at the tollbooth now for a couple of years. Maybe now he's ready to do what it takes to make it in a decent job. My job is overwhelming right now and they've authorized me to hire someone. I know I can trust Edgar. What toll-booth is he at?"

Heather rolled through the old tollbooth in a Mercedes C class. It was non-Carrera quality, which made Ari less nervous—plus Ari had always liked Heather just a bit. Edgar hung his head as she pulled up at the booth.

"Look, Edgar," said Heather. "Drew told us everything. I'm in a position at my company where I could use an assistant. It's my call entirely, so I could hire you. I work in compliance. It might be something you would like. You would be the assistant compliance direc-tor. Here's my card. Call me."

Ari once again had no say except to force Edgar to wait until 3 P.M. when his shift ended to make the call. Edgar noticed Ari's lack of enthusiasm and unusual reticence and asked, "Ari, she's in compliance. How can I possibly go wrong working there? Why you'll have nothing to do. Maybe they'll have that new Atari game there, Donkey Kong Jr."

Once again, Edgar gave notice to his supervisor, who now seemed to be ninety if he was a day. "You'll be back," was all the old man offered without even glancing up from his desk. "Why does he keep saying that?" Edgar wondered aloud to Ari. Ari shrugged, for he had no plausible explanation.

Leaving his quickly-aging tollbooth supervisor, Edgar began his work as Heather's assistant. Ari advised Edgar to wait on changing apartments. "Really, your track record for employment stability is not so good," Ari told Edgar, who, of course, was fuming.

Heather's job at WCAE, Inc., a multinational investment house with both brokerage and merger divisions, was to be certain that the employees of the company were in "compliance" with the law. She kept an eagle eye out for insider trading and traveled around the company giving presentations on what exactly insider trading was. "Anything you know that the public doesn't know can't be used for buying, selling, puts, calls, options, margin trades, leverage, or any of those other arbitrage, derivative, and financial instrument things that are the bread and butter of Wall Street," was the closing line Heather always used in her presentation. Edgar also heard Heather say the same thing when employees called her on the telephone to clarify something. "No, you can't tell your neighbor and then you and your neighbor split the profits," was one answer. "No, you can't tell your daughter, even though her married name is different," was another. Heather knew this stuff backwards and forwards and she ran a tight ship. "They always think they can come up with an angle to beat the law," she told Edgar one day.

Edgar was a fast study, soon answering questions that came in and even doing a few presentations for Heather. Edgar fit in a bit better with Heather and the work she was doing. In fact, he was feeling really good about Heather, WCAE, Inc., and even the prospect of a new apartment. Employment stability was finally his, and he was not exposed to the elements at work, a downside to the tollbooth that bothered even Ari a bit. In fact, Edgar was feeling so long term and comfortable, that he asked Heather where she lived and sought advice on apartments for himself. "Well, I live at Park Lane Apartments, but the rent is $4,800 per month. That might be a bit much for you."

Ari chimed in, "$4,800 a year and we're talking." On occasion Ari showed that a little Mrs. Vera Benchley had rubbed off on him.

Edgar sneered at Ari, but Ari was too busy mocking Edgar's meager salary to note the cause for concern in what Heather had just revealed. Edgar knew that Heather's salary was $74,000 per year. That meant she was spending all but $16,400 per year on her rent. Her taxes had to be at least $15,000. She went out to lunch every day and she wasn't skimping on the Louis Vuitton bags and they weren't the knock-offs, either. Ari soon recovered from his own witty remark long enough to follow Edgar's train of thought and added his own input to Edgar's calculations: "And I believe those are this year's Prada shoes she has on today. Come on, Ed. Put some of that accounting know-how that got you fired at the last job to work here." Ari was again quite pleased with what he viewed as razor sharp comments at Edgar's expense.

Edgar worked through the numbers and came up with the obvious conclusion about Heather's financial picture: Heather must have inherited money. "Case closed," Edgar told Ari. Ari would not be still. The new Nintendo system that Edgar had purchased for Ari and hooked up to a pitiful television in his office area had lost its charm.

"Keep your eyes peeled, my boy," was all Ari would say. "You haven't even figured in her Mercedes yet. Even if she's leasing, the payments have got to be $500 per month."

Ari had been with Edgar too long for Edgar to put Ari's thoughts out of his mind. With his eyes peeled, Edgar saw that Heather had an abundant supply of cash always on hand. And Edgar was never sure where she was and with whom she had all the luncheon meetings she scheduled nearly every day.

And Ari had taken to watching *Wall Street* on video each night with the volume loud enough to disturb Edgar but not the neighbors. Ari would rewind to see again the part when Martin Sheen lectures Charlie Sheen about the importance of making an honest dollar.

Then one day Edgar and Ari returned to the office after hours because Ari had forgotten his umbrella. Edgar had offered to share, but there was the height difference and Ari was uncomfortable slouching. Thankfully, Ari's umbrella was also invisible to most of the world, for Edgar had no idea how he would ever explain a suspended umbrella walking next to him.

Heather was still in her office. She had someone with her. Edgar couldn't see who it was, but it sounded like Drew. He wasn't up to facing Drew, so he and Ari tiptoed into the office for umbrella retrieval, though one can understand why tiptoeing on the part of Ari was superfluous.

Above the sound of the tiptoes, Edgar heard Heather say, "We're doing great. If this ever came out we'd be bigger than, what was that guy's name a few years back?—the one with insider trading? Boesky? That's it. Ivan Boesky. We'd be bigger than Ivan Boesky."

Drew added, "Except that we're smarter. Remember, we read Edgar's finance paper on insider trading. We know where all these folks messed up and we're avoiding their mistakes. That Edgar—his management paper was a disaster, but the one on insider trading, well, you can't buy term papers like that on the Internet. It had it all: content, footnotes, analysis."

"He always did work hard. Still does, working here," Heather added.

"Yeah, what a schmuck," Drew replied with a laugh that had Edgar nearly racing into the room. Thankfully, Ari restrained him.

"Not now," Ari said, "Not now."

Ari and Edgar left before they heard the end of the Drew and Heather conversation. Heather perked up for some reason when she told Drew, "I saw Elise McDonough this morning. Just like Steve said, she asked about Edgar again. When I said he worked for me, she said she would come by to visit. There's something about Edgar. Elise never says it aloud, but I think she is quite taken with him and Edgar thinks he's not worthy of her. That's just how Edgar is. And that's what Elise loves. This has all the makings of a great love story."

Drew scowled.

Ari and Edgar returned to their studio apartment and ate in silence. Edgar had a hunch about what Heather was doing. She was using all the information she had about the company to tip off others like Drew. They were then making trades in the market in advance of the public disclosure. Edgar, working out some cash flow models, figured that Heather was taking in at least an extra $15,000 per month. "Tax free," Ari added.

"What I couldn't do with $15,000 per month. That's three times what I make in salary as assistant compliance officer," Edgar muttered to Ari. "And I wouldn't have to do anything with inside information. I could just tell Heather that I know what she's doing and she could either increase my pay by that amount or I could go to the SEC," Edgar plotted. "I don't aid, abet, or participate. I just keep my mouth shut."

Ari was negotiating his chicken potpie. Still, his strain with Swanson's less-than-gourmet taste did not keep him from making his point: "Wouldn't be honest. Wouldn't be right." "Also," Ari added, "there's a state criminal code provision on extortion, the big shakedown, duress, threats, you know, Eliot Ness types of things." Edgar wondered how Ari knew these things. Ari read his mind and responded, "Easy. You wrote a paper on white-collar crimes for business law class. Remember? One of your best. You could have gone to law school kid, but I'm getting too old to see you through that profession. Don't have the legs anymore for that much pummeling."

So Edgar returned to work with Ari the next day, both pretending nothing had happened. Edgar was sure Ari's dander would be up over insider trading, but Ari held his peace. Edgar continued his work, having been assigned the arduous task of making certain that every employee had signed the compliance and ethical code agreement for the year. As he was following up with the ethical and compliance code slackers, he noticed that more of Heather's sorority sisters were calling her. Then came dinners with college friends each night, in addition to the daily luncheons. There was an ongoing stream of social engagements as well as new designer clothing. And Heather never once submitted a lunch or dinner tab for reimbursement. Edgar tried that one on Ari, "See what an honest employee she is?" Ari was as amused with Edgar's wit about as much as Edgar had been with Ari's rent comment.

It was just sixteen months into his new job, four times the amount of time at his first job with Drew, that Edgar sat down with Ari one day and asked, "Ari, I know what's going on. You remember my paper on insider trading?"

"One of your best," said Ari.

"It's only a matter of time. The SEC connects dots and people. And when one of them sings, Heather is in trouble. Then I will have been here working as her right-hand man, and who knows what they'll assume. They'll wonder how I couldn't have known. And then I'll have to put down that I worked for her and that will appear on my already deficient resume and who is going to want to call Cell Block C in Leavenworth to get my former supervisor's view on my abilities? I've seen the activity going through here. This has got to be a fairly big operation with some big dollars. The irony is she runs a great compliance program. It's just that she can't keep herself in compliance."

"Look on the bright side; you won't have to pack this time. We're still at the studio," Ari said, winding up the control wires for his Nintendo machine.

"One more thing, Ari," Edgar said with furrowed brow, "Do I need to tell anyone?"

"Not this time, my boy," Ari said. (Ari had always called Edgar "my boy" or "kid" during the elementary and junior high years, but he had not used these terms of endearment since Edgar's sophomore year in high school. Edgar was surprised by its reemergence, but somehow felt assured by it as he weighed the demands of insider trading, co-conspiracy, and the possibility of interrogation by Justice Department lawyers.) "Nope; while telling someone or not telling someone is debatable, just leave this time. She'll know anyway. Thanks to my training, you have never had a poker face."

And so Edgar gave Heather his resignation. Initially she asked, "Was it the male/female thing? Too hard to have me as your supervisor?" As she looked at Edgar's face, she could almost feel Ari's presence. "What is it about you that makes us all feel guilty? We're not bad people you know. We just do what average people do. It's just that you have never been average. Oh, maybe in your grades, but that's because you insisted on doing it all by yourself. Why is it that we all feel the need to justify what we do around you?"

"I guess I just believe in compliance," was all Edgar would say. He and Ari left.

As they boarded elevator one for their literal and figurative descent to unemployment, Elise McDonough got off elevator three, finally working in a visit with Heather and Edgar.

"You just missed him. The ingrate quit," Heather told the ever-elegant Elise.

Elise smiled.

CHAPTER 7

One More Try:
Steve Gives Edgar a Job
Sometimes the Ethical Route
Is Opportunity Knocking

Edgar and Ari were soon back at the tollbooth, just as Edgar's supervisor had predicted when he left for the job with Heather. Ari told Edgar that the tollbooth supervisor reminded him of Louie DePalma on the television series *Taxi*. Louie relished the fact that Bobby Wheeler could never quite make it in his chosen field and always had to return to being a cabbie. Bobby was always certain he was finally leaving for good and Louie was equally certain that Bobby would be back. Edgar's supervisor was taller and older, and oddly, while seeming a hundred years old, had more hair than Louie, but the sentiment was the same. He was convinced Edgar would never make it out of the tollbooth business. Edgar often wondered if Ari had some connection with the supervisor.

It was midday at the tollbooth, between the lunch crowd and rush hour, when a rather elegant Jaguar pulled into Edgar's station with a driver looking for change. It was Steve.

"Edgar, how goes the straight-arrow life? Not well, from what I hear," Steve half-shouted. Heather, Steve, and Drew had once again gathered the night before to mock Edgar's ongoing career in the tollbooth because he had such trouble holding onto the jobs they gave him.

Edgar could only respond, "I'll get you your change." Even Ari was close to a tear over the sheer indignity of it all.

"Really, Edgar, all I'm saying is you don't seem to fit well in the big corporate environment. But, I'm running my own company. I developed a product that fills a niche and it's the buzz of the industry. Everyone is waiting for its launch. I could use some help. You always have been reliable. Here's my card. I'm talking about an officer-level position, complete with stock options. Give me a call."

Edgar took the card as he gave Steve his change. Ari was standing next to Edgar's supervisor nodding as the supervisor said, "Go ahead. Call. You'll be back."

As was his custom, Edgar made the call after his shift ended. By the next day Edgar had a corner office, with his own assistant, a six-figure salary, and stock options. Ari was enormously uncomfortable, sitting as if he were a child outside the principal's office. He was even sitting on his paws, not the back ones, as surely all rabbits do, but with his front paws tucked under his back paws. He would occasionally rock back and forth and say, "If it sounds too good to be true, it is too good to be true."

But Edgar had his hands full, even if Ari's paws were not. He was in charge of budgets, financial statements, and production. In fact, Edgar wasn't at all sure what Steve was doing. Putting in fifteen-hour days, with much complaining from Ari, Edgar was able to get the budgets, financials, and production in place within six months.

Edgar had been so busy that he and Ari were still in their studio apartment. Even with six figures, Edgar had no time to find a larger place. Edgar had no time for anything. Except for rent, utilities, and food he still had all of his salary. He had invested it and it was doing nicely. His only indulgence was the Godiva "White Chocolate Raspberry" ice cream that Ari demanded since their newfound wealth. Godiva beat Swanson's hands or paws down.

With Edgar's financials in place, Steve's company was ready for its IPO. With its promising new product and production in place, Steve's company was going to the market to raise money for expansion. Edgar's financials had won the admiration of the outside auditors. Edgar had reviewed every word of the prospectus and he knew them all to be true statements about Steve, the product, and how ready the company was for multinational expansion. "Now this is the way to do business. Full disclosure. Honest. How about this, Ari?" Edgar asked.

Ari was, once again, uncharacteristically quiet. Monosyllabic even. "Great!" was all Ari could offer. Edgar had been through enough with Ari to understand that a shoe was about to drop.

Late one night as Ari read *People* and howled at its crossword puzzle's simplicity, Edgar worked away proofing the company prospectus one last time. Their work and pleasure were interrupted when an engineer from the belly of Steve's company knocked on their door.

"Excuse me, sir, but I saw your light and thought you might have a few minutes," the humble engineer said as he approached. Ari was already on his feet welcoming the young man into the office, but, of course, the young engineer had no way of knowing he was already being well received.

Edgar still saw himself as a tollbooth operator and couldn't imagine that anyone would be afraid to approach him. He stood alongside Ari and gave the young engineer a warm welcome.

Sheepishly the young engineer began: "This is not easy for me. I've been debating for weeks what to do. My wife thinks I'm crazy, but I figure if you can't sleep at night then something is really wrong. This new product is great. There's just one problem—it leaks. And you know it's not as if anyone can tell when it has leaked and even if it got on them. But, I now know that what's leaking is carcinogenic. I found some older studies on its use, and death is nearly certain in 25 percent of the cases where there's contact. There's one more problem. If it leaks around heat, even just high outdoor temperatures, it's combustible. It's almost a spontaneous thing."

Edgar could only state the obvious: "This is not good news."

But then the young engineer added, "Oh, but it's highly fixable. There's just one design adjustment, a slight retooling in production, and we got it licked for about $8 per unit. It will put the price over $100, but there is a fairly large risk here in terms of injury and liability. I can do a memo outlining the costs and benefits."

"*No!*" Edgar nearly shouted, "No memo." Edgar had written another of his infamous term papers on the Ford Pinto's exploding gas tank. He remembered all too well the rear-end collisions that resulted in death and disfigurement and the young engineer's memo in that company that had outlined the costs of fixing the exploding gas tank versus the cost of human life. The memo became Exhibit I in all of the product liability cases. He also remembered that the state of Indiana had indicted Ford for manslaughter. And he had just read about another such memo by another young engineer at GM, only this time it was a Malibu.

Ari remembered the term paper and the Pinto as well. "Remember I told you to put in that paragraph about the memo sealing Ford's fate?" Ari said. "Remember how I told you to include the discussion about the engineer's responsibility? And do you remember the paragraph on the executive who gave the go-ahead for production and sales without making even one of the engineer's repairs? What did you write there?"

"I wrote that the executive bore the ultimate responsibility and should have fixed the car, held up production, and priced the Pinto slightly above the target of under $3,000. But, really, Ari, I didn't know how much money the guy was making and that his career hung in the balance. If I do this, I'm zero for three. I will have lost three jobs right in succession—jobs where I worked for friends and still managed to get myself fired. I'm forty years old, spent the bulk of my working life in a tollbooth with a geezer for a supervisor, and haven't held down a real job for more than two years. Heck, I can't even list a reference for anyone I've worked for except at the tollbooth," Edgar said in soliloquy fashion.

"Yes, but remember back at Zenon when you went to the vice president after you saw Drew and then wrote to the CEO? Remember how you felt when you were rejected out-of-hand?" said Ari, now breaking into a full-blown pace.

Edgar realized he was, for the first time, talking aloud to Ari in the presence of another person. But the young engineer, who had not seen Ari greet him, seemed unfazed. He then leaned over Edgar's desk and said, "It's okay. I see him too. I didn't see him when I first came in, but maybe he joined us while I wasn't looking." Ari looked at the young engineer and said simply, "Thank you for noticing. There are so few of you."

So, there they were—the three musketeers. All for one and one for all, whatever it was they were for. Edgar and the young engineer were uncertain why they were the only ones in the world who could see and hear Ari, and they spoke aloud of their puzzlement.

Ari chimed in: "It's not that others don't see or hear me. It's that they see or hear me once and ignore me. I can't take rejection. I can take a good fight and Edgar here has given me a heck of a marathon, but he always comes around and he's never lost sight of me."

"What now?" asked the young engineer.

Edgar knew there was no turning back. He had not only the potential of an old-fashioned Ari pummeling (Ari was intransigent where human life was involved, as Edgar recalled from the days of the back seat of the Polara)—but also a flesh-and-bones thorn in his side in the form of a young engineer. "I'll talk to Steve in the morning," he assured. "Don't say anything and hold up on your work until I can see this thing through."

Then Edgar, Ari, and the young engineer left. The young engineer headed to an apartment building more pitiful than that of Edgar and Ari. Edgar and Ari went home, and as they ate some benign oven concoction together Ari noted, "Good thing we have a lease here."

"Looks like we'll be staying," said Edgar. He thought he should call the tollbooth supervisor that night, but even Ari encouraged him to hold out hope for Steve. Still, as Ari settled in for the night, he told Edgar, "I shall miss the Godiva ice cream."

The next morning, Edgar ventured into Steve's office with the engineer's drawings, the crunched numbers, and a proposal for new pricing with a delayed production schedule. Steve was on the phone with his architect. He and his wife were building a 6,200 square-foot home in a tony new gated community.

"I don't care what it costs. I need the eight-car garage. And one should have a hydraulic lift," were the instructions Steve was bellowing. As he hung up, he motioned for Edgar to approach and said, "You know me and cars, I want plenty and I want them kept inside." Edgar found it hard to relate, having just progressed from the Corolla he had had since college to an Accord.

"I'm not sure where to begin, Steve, but there's a problem with the product's international launch," was Edgar's beginning phrase.

"Well, that's the kind of phrase that's right up there with, 'Steve, you have a huge lump we can't explain,' or 'Steve, you'll never be able to drive again,' or 'Steve, your wife is leaving you,'" Steve joked with Edgar.

Edgar proceeded to explain the leak, the danger, the combustibility, and the fix. Steve asked, "Who told you this?" Edgar explained it was a young engineer, and Steve responded, "Fire him and purge his computer."

Ari was on the edge of his seat. He loved drama. Actually, Ari loved tension in the air that he had helped create and for which he had absolutely no accountability. This was the best drama and tension Ari had ever experienced in his time with Edgar.

"I can't and I won't. If you are going to fire someone, then fire me. I'm the one who brought it to you," was Edgar's response, which stunned Ari. Ari had not given Edgar any hint about what to do. Indeed, Edgar could have very well been confused by the smile on Ari's face. It was the smile of enjoying the confrontation, though it could have been easily misinterpreted by a novice. But Edgar was clearly no longer a novice. In fact, Ari was finding his life with Edgar terribly unchallenging—Edgar was always doing the right thing these days. But he wouldn't dare tell Edgar that just yet, as he felt Edgar still needed the mental pummelings on occasion. "The lad is not quite confident enough," Ari would often say to himself. And here Ari was witnessing a turning point. "My boy," Ari thought to himself with pride, "My boy."

Steve thought for a moment and then said, "Edgar, don't push me on this. The investment banker is ready to go. The marketing plan and distribution system are in place."

"Ah, that's what he does that I don't do—marketing and distribution," thought Edgar.

"If we pull the plug now, this company and this product are dead. You've read the buzz out there. We are *it*, buddy. It's now or never.

It's either launch or fold." Steve appeared to be running out of both platitudes, metaphors, and all manner of speech designed to convince Edgar to proceed without changing anything.

"But Steve, it's not worth it. If we launch and the leaks start, we've lost it all anyway, and in a much more public way with a great deal more liability. Not to mention the risk we place our customers in. We're talking about possible loss of life here, Steve," as Edgar became more forceful.

"Atta boy, Edgar," was Ari's only observation.

"For once in your life, Edgar, be reasonable. Get off your soapbox and think like a businessman. Play with the team. Don't stop the game. Do you ever see the impact of doing things your way? What about our employees? What about their mortgages? What about their children? The way I see it, we cut them off because you and some inexperienced engineer think our product might have a problem. Give it a rest, Edgar. Give it a rest, and go with me on this one."

"You know I can't," was all Edgar could say.

"And you know I have to fire you. The product launch and the IPO go forward with you or without you. Do you realize what you're giving up with those stock options? Edgar, you could be a multimillionaire within weeks if you just hang in there with me," said Steve, now appearing to be pleading.

Edgar simply said, "I'll have my desk cleaned out before noon."

As Edgar walked out, he made his customary scan of the room for Ari because Ari was often distracted and not always clear on the decorum and importance of leaving on cue. When Edgar returned to his office, he found Ari already there, rather oddly sitting in Edgar's chair.

"When I told you that I would miss the Godiva ice cream, I didn't mean because I knew Steve wouldn't relent. It was because I knew you wouldn't. I've trained you, Edgar boy. Although I should probably call you 'Edgar man.' I'm moving on," was all that Ari offered from behind Edgar's desk.

"You mean you're not going back to the tollbooth with me?" pleaded Edgar. The words stunned Edgar himself. Since the fifth grade he had wanted Ari out of his life. Now that his dream was coming true, he found that he didn't want Ari to go.

"Nope, no tollbooth for me. In fact, it's not the tollbooth for you, either. Take that young engineer with you—you know I was thinking of hanging with him for a while, but at this point he's about as much of a challenge as you are. Hire that supervisor from the tollbooth and start your own company. You could be a consultant on compliance. You could be an auditor who ferrets out fraud. Or you could find the fix for Steve's product's flaw that's going to toss him into Chapter 7 bankruptcy. You can buy him out and take it from there," was Ari's sage advice.

"And what will I use for collateral? My Accord?" said Edgar.

"Why not? It's about what this company will be worth once the information you and the young engineer have gets out there," said the very relaxed Ari, "and you're going to have to trust me on this one. You have no idea what's out there just waiting for you."

Ari stood up, gave Edgar a slap on the side of the arm with his paw, and said, "See you, chief." Ari had picked up a certain lingo from watching one too many David Letterman shows. "And one more thing—be sure to talk to our supervisor from the tollbooth."

"I thought I wasn't going back there," Edgar protested.

"You're not, but he can help," was all Ari said before taking his Game Boy and leaving.

"Right, a 190-year-old coot who has spent his life in state government can help me launch a business?" thought Edgar.

"I heard that!" Ari shouted back. "Where's the trust?" he thought.

CHAPTER 8

Edgar Starts His Own Company

The Ethical Finish First Eventually, and with Peace of Mind

dgar was alone in his studio apartment that night—alone for the first time in three decades. There was no Ari, but there was a knock at the door. It would have been unlike Ari to knock, but Edgar was hopeful. With his Swanson *du jour* getting cold, Edgar leaped to the door, not as quickly as Ari could have, but a respectable leap nonetheless.

There at the door of the studio apartment was the humble young engineer. "Heard you quit. Actually, I heard you got fired," he said.

"What possible difference could it make? After having had three jobs, I still can't get a reference," Edgar mused.

"Well, this I'm certain of, I quit," said the young engineer. Then he paused, "Where is he?"

"You mean Ari?" said Edgar. "Well, he left me."

"He left you because you did the right thing?"

"Yes, he left me because he trained me to do the right thing and he said I didn't need him any longer. He said he had to move along to the more ethically challenged."

"You must miss him," the young engineer said sadly.

Edgar did miss Ari, but he invited the young engineer inside and together, over some Godiva "White Chocolate Raspberry," they hatched a plan.

"Ari was right. When this thing starts leaking, it won't be isolated. Companies will need repairs and Steve will have to declare bankruptcy. We can repair these things and then take over the company in bankruptcy and make this thing work and work safely," said Edgar, as his mind raced ahead of his words.

"I'm not much with accounting, but don't we need money?"

"As luck would have it, I've been too busy to spend any of the money Steve was paying me. I've stashed nearly all of my salary and it has been invested in this bull market, so it's enough to get started. And I know this guy in the State Department of Transportation who has been looking to retire and work in business. He's got mechanical expertise. He might be a good production guy."

Suddenly Edgar realized what he had said. "Of course," he thought. "The old guy at the tollbooth had always been tinkering with products. He was always fixing and repairing. He had told Edgar once that he could fix anything and did so for folks in his garage nearly every night and throughout his weekends. He'd mentioned once that he would start a fix-it shop when he retired." Ari was right as usual.

So, Edgar took his savings, the young engineer, and his now-retired supervisor from the tollbooth and started a company. For two years they did repairs on Steve's leaky product out of Edgar's studio apartment. Edgar switched from Swanson to Kroger potpies to keep the company afloat. But business was coming in, slowly but steadily.

Steve's Company Enters Bankruptcy

Ethical Indiscretions Haunt the Sprinters

ithin one week of the IPO, Steve's net worth had reached $20 million. Within one year from the product launch, the product liability class-action suits had begun. Within two years, there were so many lawsuits that the external auditors would no longer certify Steve's financials as those of an ongoing entity. Without outside auditor certification, Steve had to take his company into Chapter 7 bankruptcy. Edgar was waiting with some cash and an Accord. He purchased the plant, the designs, and the assets for a song.

Steve was facing a criminal investigation for his failure to disclose the information about the leaks to the underwriter, in the prospectus, and to OSHA. As it turned out, someone had found a memo in Steve's files about the leak. At the end of the memo was a handwritten note, "Why do you think Edgar left the company? He wasn't fired!"

Edgar needed money to get production of the new and unflawed design rolling, and he was tapped out. The capital budget for repairing products out of a studio apartment was nothing compared to what was needed for a factory. He needed to do a stock offering and he had zero credibility in the business community, or so he thought.

"How does a guy who has never been able to hold a job manage to raise capital for his own business?" Edgar worried.

Edgar shopped his idea around to investment bankers and there were no takers. He had one last appointment to pitch his idea, company, and product. When he arrived for the appointment, Edgar was stunned to find that the investment banker assigned to review his proposal was the former vice president of Drew's company—the one who had given Edgar the "be a team player" lecture when Edgar had taken his numbers and FASBs in to raise issues about accounting improprieties. When Edgar saw who it was, he pivoted on his heel and said, "Sorry to have wasted your time."

But as he was headed out the door, the former Zenon division VP–turned–investment banker leaped from behind the desk. Not an Ari leap, but a respectable one nonetheless.

"No, wait. You don't understand. I left just days after the CEO fired you. It was the strangest thing. I couldn't let go of what you said. I kept hearing, 'Wouldn't be honest. Wouldn't be right.' So, with my wife in a near state of clinical depression, I walked away from all those options, all that salary, and all those perks. But, I've never forgotten you, Edgar. When the firm got your letter of inquiry, it found its way to my desk. I'm not sure why. I never handle IPOs, and I surely don't handle companies your size, but I knew your name. We're ready to do business with you. We even know the whole Steve story. Same thing—you walked away from that, too!

"I told my partners, 'This guy you can trust. If this thing fails, he'd pay you back, even if he has to work in a tollbooth until he is ninety-five—and I understand he has a guy like that working in his company—some tollbooth supervisor who retired and has a mechanical knack.' They were a little worried about that last part because your entire mechanical expertise is tied up with a guy we hear talks to himself, mumbling something like Ari Onassis or some such name."

"I knew it," Edgar thought. "Ari was tight with the tollbooth supervisor."

There in that office, with the former division VP who had once maligned Edgar, Tortoise Enterprises began. The rest, as they say, is history.

But something else also began in that same office. As Edgar was signing the paperwork for his IPO, he looked to his right as the private door to the former division VP's office opened. Edgar had to look twice because the first time he looked up and to the right, he would have sworn he saw Elise McDonough standing there smiling at him. Now a man who has spent most of his life living with and speaking to a rabbit the size of John Wayne whom no one else sees is bound to doubt the appearance of visions, especially a vision as lovely as the elegant Elise McDonough. There's a certain hesitancy about acknowledging visions of any type when you've spent decades with a pummeling, political pooka.

But when Edgar looked a second time, he saw that it was indeed Elise McDonough, and not only was she smiling, she spoke, "Edgar, the proposal didn't just end up on his desk. I put it there. This is where I work. I would have approved it in the blink of an eye, but I didn't want your first stock offering to carry a taint."

"What taint would it carry if you approved it?" a nervous Edgar, still worried that he might again be speaking to an illusion, asked.

"The taint of a girlfriend approving an IPO for her inexperienced boyfriend. I knew that would upset you. I've watched you all my life. I've never known a more honorable and conflicts-free person, so I made sure, for your sake, that it was all done on the up-and-up and completely independently," the elegant Elise explained.

"But, I'm not your boyfriend," Edgar stammered.

Elise McDonough just smiled.

C H A P T E R   1 0

More Sighs, but Triumphs

Success Comes from Doing What's Honest and Right

Our story began with Edgar sighing at his desk at Tortoise. Edgar didn't sigh because Ari was forcing him to do what was "honest" and "right." It had been years since he and Ari had parted ways. Edgar sighed because he still fought the battle, with his employees, with his children, with his bankers, and with his board. There wasn't a day that went by when Edgar didn't have some meeting in which he was restraining someone with Ari's advice, "Wouldn't be honest. Wouldn't be right."

He sighed because it was so hard. He sighed because it was such a battle. And he sighed because it always seemed like it would be so much easier to just give in and be like the rest of them.

But the real source of Edgar's sigh this morning was that he had learned that Heather had been indicted on eighteen felony counts for everything from securities fraud to wire fraud to RICO to money laundering. The SEC finally caught up with one of her sorority sisters who had done some fancy trading on a company's stock just prior to its announcement of a merger with its competitor, and Heather's company had been handling the merger. Heather and the sorority sister had exchanged information over lunch and the sorority sister, who really was not one of Heather's brighter friends, sang like a canary when confronted by the SEC. She not only named Heather as her source, she named everyone else she knew to whom Heather was selling information for some hefty fees per tip. She also spilled her guts about Heather's ill-gotten term papers and even told the Department of Justice and the Scholastic Aptitude Testing Division about the memory pegs and AP history. It was a real cleansing of the soul for the sorority sister.

Over the years, Heather had amassed close to $5 million by selling inside information to a multitude of college friends. She had even taken to selling information to friends of friends and then on to friends of friends of friends. However, the IRS, the SEC, and the Department of Justice had seized those funds. Even Heather's 401(k) was a goner. Heather couldn't even afford a studio apartment. She was living with her father, who was springing for her defense lawyer and reminding her daily of his contribution with one more dig: "Why couldn't you have been more like Edgar, instead of taking after Steve and Drew?"

"Drew?" Edgar thought when he heard the story of Heather's irritated father, "what happened with Drew?" For this information he turned to his investment banker.

"I can't believe you didn't hear," was his response, "Drew went to prison about five years ago. He has two more to go. Turned out that the CEO let him take the fall for all that accounting mumbo jumbo you told me about. The CEO denied that he knew anything. In fact, the CEO said that Drew did it to get his bonuses and options to support his lifestyle—you know, the Carerra, the travel, the women. And the CEO had credibility with the prosecutors because he had dredged up all kinds of information on Drew. He had him cold on buying term papers in college and even a Mr. Gallinger from high school came forward and told about some elaborate scheme he never cracked on cheating in AP History. The guy looked like a life-long cheat and the CEO beat the rap. You know Drew was only doing what the CEO told him to do. In fact, that's how Drew got promoted so quickly and why the CEO kept him around. Last I heard, he was doing seminars in prison for students of business ethics along the lines of 'Don't you dare make my mistakes. I didn't do what was honest. I didn't do what was right. Remember, this career of yours is a marathon, not a sprint.'"

And so Edgar sighed. Why had he been the lucky one? Why had he been graced with Ari? How was it that no one else saw Ari? And how did he manage to be successful?

When Edgar turned around from his window to his desk, he was stunned and delighted to see Ari lounging on the sofa. Edgar was surprised that Ari had returned. He was more surprised that Ari was not at the video game table that Edgar had purchased for old times' sake, as a reminder of Ari.

"It's an easy answer, sport," said Ari. "Sport" was a new term. Ah, the modern Ari. "You did what was right. You did what was honest. It just takes time, pal." Another new term of endearment, "pal." Edgar sensed Ari was watching way too much Letterman still. "Hanging in there with the guts to see it through— that's what it takes."

How good it was to see Ari after all these years. "Are you here because you're worried about me again?" asked Edgar.

"Nope, but I have to tell you, you and Elise, well, you've got a son with serious issues. Hard to believe he comes from you two with your gene pools. I may have to revisit my nature versus nurture theories. You know what I think of Elise, impeccable character and all that, and she did it without my help. But, out of respect for his father, and because I spent a little time with his father during the formative years, I'll be hanging out with him for a while. In fact, he may take longer than his father—the times are rough for honesty and doing what's right. But, you know he'll make it. Just be patient during his tollbooth–studio apartment days. He'll get there."

Edgar wasn't worried at all. But he might want to have his son spend less time with Grandma Vera Benchley, because she was still trying to get new pairs of glasses for free. Without some assistance, the acorn doesn't fall far from the tree.

Thoughts on Edgar, Ari, and Winning in the Long Run

10 Pointers for Playing by the Rules

(Courtesy of Ari)

1. Honesty is a tough thing.
2. Playing by the rules means living with an occasional setback.
3. Doing the right thing often means more work.
4. Being ethical sometimes means running behind in the race.
5. Expect a little mockery for playing ethically.
6. Being ethical means you have to speak up.
7. Sometimes the ethical route is opportunity knocking.
8. The ethical finish first eventually, and with peace of mind.
9. Ethical indiscretions haunt the sprinters.
10. Success comes from doing what's honest and right.

"I would never suggest that ethics is simple. Not only does one have to know the right thing to do—one must also have the fortitude to do it."

— Norman R. Augustine
Former Chairman, Lockheed Martin

Why Ari's System Is Different and Works

Ari offered Edgar an ethics system: "Wouldn't be honest. Wouldn't be right." Some system! That kind of system would be a tough sell in the field of business ethics, philosophy, or, for that matter, to some clergy. Even Dr. Phil might dismiss it. What businesspeople are often looking for is a system that gives them the answer they *want*, not necessarily the answer that is honest or right. They're looking to exert minimal effort when it comes to ethics, and, if possible, want nothing too taxing on the conscience. There is a faulty assumption floating in the business atmosphere that "ethics in business" and "success in business" are mutually exclusive functions. So, ethics be damned, get the money, the fame, etc. ASAP.

The Folly of Codes, Compliance, and Training Programs

Nevertheless, you have to ease the conscience into such an approach to business. Corporate compliance programs offer comfort. Codes of ethics, in their three-color brochure glory, are a source of pride, "We've got ethics. We wrote them down right here in this code. Also, we have clever reminders on our desks about the ethics hotline."

Some companies offer ethics training. "Come sit and discuss ethical theory with us," the high-salaried consultants will state, "and see if it has any application in this company." Employees then return to their desks covered with decorative and ethical reminders in order to get on with the business of cooking the books. Compliance programs do not stand in the way of what FASB interpretations allow.

Ethical Models' Facile Silliness

An Associated Press story on the upswing in business school ethics courses in the post-Enron era included this observation: "The point, professors say, is not to teach students right and wrong but to give them a framework for making ethical decisions amid the uncertainty of business."[1] With this much latitude on ethics, step aside Andrew Fastow and Bernie Ebbers, your scams are small potatoes. To paraphrase Janis Joplin, "framework" is just another word for nothing left that is unethical.

These frameworks and models are the salve for the conscience that enable the desired decisions to be made without the accompanying guilt. These models are not Ari and Edgar's way. Edgar's story is one of discomfort and defiant honesty. Ethics is not always comfortable, at least initially, and there's nothing wishy-washy about being honest and doing right.

Spend enough time in the squishy territory of these codes and ethics models and you'll find yourself trotting down a path of company destruction seen previously only in Old Testament stories of wrath. The Enron officers did not arise one day and exclaim, "You know what would be good? A gigantic fraud of off-the-books partnerships in which we hold an interest and profit mightily all while keeping the share price high!" No, what Andrew Fastow and "Andy's boys," as those who worked with Enron's CFO were called, decided was that the best way to maintain shareholder value, keep Enron's employees employed (complete with concierge), and benefit most of

Houston's philanthropic community, was to transfer Enron's debts off the books and leverage Enron to the max.[2]

The only drawback was that Enron's, WorldCom's, Tyco's, and others' financial statements were, well, just not honest or right, though they were in full compliance with FASB, AICPA, GAAP, and most ethical models. And we all issued a gigantic, coast-to-coast, "Tsk! Tsk!" We don't care about legalities. We know what's honest and right and it's something more than the levels of *actus reus* and *mens rea* required under the United States Code, Titles 15 or 18,[3] and any other number of penal codes or accounting code acronyms. Honest and right are something more than just compliance with the law.

Why Ari's System Is Hard

So, why didn't the bright officers of Enron, WorldCom, their auditors, analysts, and even business writers stand and shout, "This isn't honest! This isn't right!"? Most at least had some questions. Enron employees circulated a humorous memo that raised concerns about the fact that Enron had created 942 companies in one year. The title of the memo was "Top Ten Reasons Enron Restructures So Frequently."[4] One of the reasons given: "Because the basic business model is to keep the outside investment analysts so confused that they will not be able to figure out that we don't know what we're doing."[5]

The folks at Enron saw the ethical issues and knew that what they were doing was neither honest nor right. But, they also had the comfortable assurance that they were in full compliance with most ethical models, keeping a good part of Houston employed and its philanthropic community endowed, not to mention the Astros appropriately housed in Enron (now Minute Maid) Field. Cooking the books seems justified. Why, Mrs. Vera Benchley would have done no less than Fastow.

So why do we now grab our pitchforks, ready to storm the Enron castle? If we were to speak honestly about ethics, and it is a topic that screams out for honesty, the bottom line is that most people understand what Ari means when he says, "Wouldn't be honest. Wouldn't be right." Models and compliance programs have mucked up the issues so much that we have trouble slogging our ways through business with ethics. We're all ethical in theory, but the practice can be a bear, or some other form of animal life, as Ari showed. Perhaps some animal form less foreboding for Wall Streeters would be better.

In the movie *Scent of a Woman*, Al Pacino plays Lt. Col. Frank Slade, a blind and retired military man grappling with reflections that he has made some awfully poor ethical decisions throughout his life. Near the end of the movie he states, "I have come to the crossroads in my life. I always knew what the right path was. Without exception, I knew. But I never took it. You know why? It was too damn hard."

Ethics is hard, but we're still outraged when we're on the receiving end of conduct that isn't honest or right. When we cover ethics cases in MBA classes, I demand of my students, "Where is the outrage?" I want outrage because outrage forces us to look within to find that part of us that says, "I don't want to be treated this way."

But knowing the solution to an ethical dilemma is only a small part of the battle. Acting on it is the challenge. That's why Ari was created. Ari is the ethical nerve to say, "No!" Ari is the still, small voice. Ari is conscience. Ari is the nagging feeling that doesn't go away when we cross that line and do what's dishonest and wrong. The distinct feature of Ari's system is finding the courage to do what Ari forced Edgar to do through physical force in the early years, and by simply being a pest in the later ones.

Doing what's honest and right is hard, but we still can't let go of right and wrong, and it never lets go of us. Even Heather saw something in Edgar that she admired and longed to have. It's the fortitude to speak up that gives us fits.

And businesspeople are not always receptive to what's honest and right. We can discuss marketing plans and failures and financial structure and changes. We are very vocal at retreats and in strategic planning, perhaps even volunteering to be the scribe for the big flip charts in the sessions. But ethics, well, that's a sensitive subject. Ethics is June and Ward Cleaver or William Bennett, and no one believes the first two ever really existed and most wish the latter would go away—he's a great deal like Ari with his reminders on these absolutes of right and wrong.

Raising an ethical issue at work is just slightly more acceptable than discussing Preparation H. People leave the room and from that moment will never look at the Preparation H discussant in quite the same way. You might as well have Edgar's haircut from the fifth grade. You are an outcast.

But Ari taught us that Edgar's choices, in the long run, made him successful while his ethically challenged friends found themselves in minimum security facilities and/or bankruptcy. Edgar's story is no different from the stories of a million businesses and even more individuals. Ari helped Edgar find the courage to say, "NO!"; to leave gainful employment; and even to make Mrs. Vera Benchley toe the line, Edgar's earliest ethical challenge in life, which began in the back seat of a Polara.

Whether in a boardroom or in the middle of a gossipy conversation that has turned ugly, it takes courage to cry, "It isn't honest. It isn't right." Ari made it impossible for Edgar to resist. We all can't have an Ari, despite the fact that life would be so lovely with him, with or without the Godiva "White Chocolate Raspberry." These pages explore Ari's system of courage. Ari's system offers a rich look at business history to help us understand that the road to good ethics is paved with a great many setbacks, detours, and even some mockery. Ari's system also teaches that the good guys, as defined by honesty and right over wrong, do finish first. Ari's good guys just take a bit longer to get there, and when they arrive, there are no federal prosecutors waiting in the wings. Ari's system is along the lines of Auntie Mame's view of life. Life's a banquet and most poor souls are starving. Long-term business success starts with ethics and most poor souls are still trying to cheat their way to the top.

Ari's system offers ten pointers on leading the ethical life. Actually, they're pointers for ethical courage to help you feel the annoying feet of a giant rabbit that will not stop kicking you until you speak up. The ten pointers will give you the illusion of the carrot- or Godiva-laden breath of an eight-foot-tall rabbit breathing down your neck as you debate whether to speak up, forever hold your peace, or at least remain silent until federal prosecutors come around and offer you a deal in exchange for singing like a canary.[6]

Ari has a system that works for any person, business, or organization. When I taught Ari's system to the MBA for Executives class at Arizona State University, I found most of them on their cell phones in the building stairwells phoning instructions to their employees, "Halt!" they were saying. They had found their gumption and stopped some of their own freight trains to Club Feds around the country. While Ari's system may not reach the infiltration levels of the Tae Bo videos, you have a guarantee that you'll break a good sweat once in a while as you work your way through to the bravado of Edgar.

"Honesty: the best of all lost arts."

—Mark Twain

"Oh, what times! Oh, what standards!"

—Cicero

I. Honesty Is a Tough Thing

As Edgar's story unfolds, you find yourself thinking, "Poor guy," or perhaps even "Pitiful guy," and some of you were even saying aloud, "Schmuck!" In the initial stages of the story, before you know the outcome, you find yourself thinking, "Why does Edgar bother? Doesn't he know the world has gone the other way?" You're right, of course, in thinking that the world has moved away from honesty and the right thing. We're nearly shockproof as the corporate earnings restatements, indictments, and revelations appear each day. That so many fall short of honesty is not, however, reason to abandon it. Honesty is a tough thing; don't forget that.

Stats on honesty show it to be a rare commodity. Only the era immediately preceding the fall of the Roman Empire was comparable. Of course, they didn't have the Internet for students to plagiarize research papers—though there are some who refer to it as peer-to-peer intellectual exchanges. Edgar coped with Ari's disapproval of memory pegs, and we cope with Internet lingo for cheating.

The Story on the Difficulty of Honesty

Edgar's challenges with honesty began at a very young age and continued throughout his life. Edgar may be fictional, but his experiences were authentic. Grade school children are less honest at home than at school and not much better at being honest at school. The 2002 survey of the Josephson Institute, a nonprofit organization that specializes in character education for children in grades K–12,[7] found:

- Ninety-three percent have lied to their parents during the past year.

- Eighty-three percent confess to lying to their teachers at school (with 63 percent saying they have done so two or more times).

- Seventy-four percent say they have cheated at school.[8]

- Forty-one percent of male children and 38 percent of female children say they have shoplifted in the past year.

- Thirty-seven percent say they would lie to get a job (more on this figure in the adult world stats).

Moguls who cheat did not develop their skills overnight. Ari intervened with Edgar while he was young, to shape him and mold him. With children, the importance of being honest and doing right needs to be taught early.

Heather, Drew, and Steve took the habits of their youth into the workplace, and they are fairly typical. The following revelations about resumes were discovered following research on 7,000 resumes by an executive search firm:[9]

- Seventy-one percent misrepresented the number of years in previous jobs.

- Sixty-four percent exaggerated their accomplishments.

- Sixty percent exaggerated the size of the organization they managed.

- Fifty-two percent indicated a partial degree as a completed degree.

- Forty-eight percent exaggerated compensation.

The figure for the number of people who misrepresent holding a Ph.D. degree is 70 percent, and studies in the medical field indicate that 20–25 percent of physicians' resumes have at least one major fabrication.[10] Although, many would refer to these exaggerations as "puffing," a rose by any other name still smells.

The most recent ethics-in-the-workplace survey has an eerie quality to it because it sounded as if the respondents were trying to reach out and have us understand that there was a problem.

Oddly, the public accounting firm of KPMG conducted the survey:[11]

- Seventy-six percent of employees have seen a high level of illegal or unethical conduct on the job during the past year.

- Forty-nine percent felt that if the public knew of the misconduct in their organizations that the result would be that the organizations would "significantly lose public trust."

- The most common ethical violations are deceptive sales practices and the disclosure of nonpublic information to the public.

The employees were telling us, "Honesty is a tough thing." They were adding, "We are not doing so well at it. You out there have no idea." A survey of CFOs, CEOs, controllers, and other top executives conducted in 1996 found that 47 percent of the top executives, 41 percent of the controllers, and 76 percent of graduate-level business students were "willing to commit fraud by understating write-offs that cut into their companies' profits."[12] And 14 percent of the CEOs and 8 percent of the controllers were willing to inflate sales figures so as to meet announced earnings expectations.[13]

The honesty thing is tough for CEOs. It's not that they don't believe in honesty, because a 2002 survey of executives found that 72 percent believe that honesty is as important now in business as it has ever been and 28 percent believe it is more important than ever.[14] However, 82 percent also confess that they are less than honest on their golf scorecards. At the same time, 82 percent also hate those who cheat at golf, and 72 percent believe that behavior on the golf course parallels behavior in business, which doesn't quite explain why 99 percent believe they themselves are honest in business even as they are dishonest at golf. All in all, the only sense to be made from the data is that executives lie in golf and lie in business but also lie about lying in business.[15] Jeff Harper, former president of Summit National Bank in Fort Worth, Texas, says that he has declined loans after golfing with CEOs because, "When you see what they'll do for a $10 bet, it makes you wonder what they'd do on a million-dollar loan."[16]

But there are other schools of thought on the issue. CEO Mark Fasciano of FatWire Software theorizes that we should be suspicious of CEOs who *don't* cheat at golf. He reasons that if they are that good at golf they are spending too much time on the greens and not enough at the company. There's a sincere sort of Vera Benchley logic in this analysis. Honesty is tough, but perhaps not as tough as following the logic of cheaters.

Warren Buffett has long compared golf cheating to financial reporting transparency and has written, "In golf, my score is frequently below par on a pro forma basis. I have firm plans to restructure my putting stroke and therefore only count the swings I take before reaching the green."[17]

So there you have it, from home to grade school and right up on through resumes and over to the golf course, it's a dream world for cheaters. There is a great deal of dishonesty going on out there. But, don't lose hope. Remember, Ari has a system for ethics. You have stats for the battle's harsh reality. But, you need some patience. Wait, as someone we know and love once said, "You'll see."

Honesty is tough, but it does have its rewards.

Putting Ari in Action

◆ Don't establish your ethics by what everyone else is doing; everyone else is often not doing what is honest or right.

◆ Stay the course on doing what's honest and right even though the world has declining standards.

◆ Teach your children well, not as Mrs. Vera Benchley did.

■■

"Good intentions are not a substitute for good actions."
—Jon Entine, former NBC television producer
and expert on social responsibility

II. Playing by the Rules Means Living with an Occasional Setback

Our hero, Edgar, did not have occasional setbacks. He had regular setbacks. In fact, Edgar would be like the player in a gigantic game of

Chutes and Ladders who always ends up falling down the slide that is the length of the board. Were life Candyland, he would end up back in Molasses Swamp, yearning for the Candy Castle territory. Monopoly? Always landing on Boardwalk when it has a hotel owned by another player.

Setbacks go hand-in-hand with honesty because, again, honesty is a tough thing. But those setbacks are temporary. Courage often requires taking a long view, having an understanding that there are occasional setbacks in living the "Ari and Edgar" way. Here is one example from business illustrating that doing what's honest and right often brings a harsh, albeit temporary, reality. Herewith, a real-life Edgar to ponder and perhaps wonder aloud whether he had his own Ari.

The Story on Living with Setbacks

Jerome J. LiCari, Ph.D., a chemist by training, was the director of research and development for Beech-Nut Nutrition Corporation in the late 1970s and early 1980s. At that time, Beech-Nut was at the cusp of national market prominence. Beech-Nut was the second-largest baby food producer in the United States and was coming as close as any company has ever come to giving number one Gerber a run for its money. LiCari's close watch on quality was one of the keys to Beech-Nut's market success. The *New York Times* rated Beech-Nut baby apple juice as the best-tasting juice on the market.[18] This was a company on a roll.

But Dr. LiCari was nervous about a contract with a new supplier, the Interjuice Trading Corporation (also known as the Universal Juice Corporation), for apple juice concentrate, a critical component in Beech-Nut's apple juice and applesauce and the natural sweetener in about 20 percent of all of Beech-Nut's baby food products. In Dr. LiCari's mind the price was too low. But that price was a huge break for Beech-Nut. Buying concentrate at a price that was 20 percent below the going market rate was its profit margin.[19]

Dr. LiCari took his suspicions, went to Beech-Nut's director of operations, John Lavery, and explained his concerns. Lavery sent two Beech-Nut employees to the Interjuice plant to inspect operations and all they found was a warehouse with no blending operations— a mighty suspicious thing for an apple concentrate supplier. Worried, Lavery required Interjuice to sign a "hold-harmless agreement" but did continue the contract.

By this time, Dr. LiCari and his staff had information from other companies that the concentrate was "almost pure corn syrup." There was no fruit in the fruit juice concentrate. Lavery reminded Dr. LiCari that the company was under tremendous economic pressure and that he had no intention of switching from the low-priced Interjuice contract unless Dr. LiCari and his staff could "prove in a court of law" that the concentrate Beech-Nut was buying was adulterated.

In 1981, Dr. LiCari went to Neils Hoyvald, the CEO of Beech-Nut. Hoyvald promised action, but some months later nothing had been done and Dr. LiCari resigned. Dr. LiCari wrote an anonymous letter to the Food and Drug Administration (FDA) disclosing the Interjuice problem. LiCari signed the letter "Johnny Appleseed," intending to remain anonymous.

Dr. LiCari, the honest one, was out of a job, and one envisions him alongside Edgar in a tollbooth somewhere in Canajoharie, New York, Beech-Nut's headquarters. He finds himself there because what Beech-Nut was doing wasn't honest or right. Losing your job is a bit of a setback.

But it's not over. In 1986, Beech-Nut, Hoyvald, and Lavery were indicted for the sale of adulterated juice products and misbranding. Beech-Nut entered a guilty plea to the felony charges and paid a $2 million fine.[20] Lavery was convicted on all counts and Hoyvald eventually entered a guilty plea.[21] Beech-Nut lost substantial market share and has not regained the position it held prior to the cost shortcut of the fake apple juice. As for Dr. LiCari, he is now a successful chemist who is doing well. It's an Ari and Edgar tale.

Dr. LiCari hung in there with one simple conviction: Selling apple juice that wasn't really apple juice wasn't honest or right. He was willing to weather the storms of speaking up and leaving his job because he knew the consequences of not doing so would be harsh. When tempted to do an unethical act, remember the consequences are expensive and tough to recover from. On the other hand, those who speak up go on to bigger and better things. The courage to act comes from remembering the costs of dishonesty and the rewards of being honest. Edgar weathered the setbacks because Ari knew what the outcome would be in the long run. But now you know Ari's secret.

Putting Ari in Action

- Doing what's right and honest almost always brings a temporary setback.

- Rewards for doing what's honest and right take time to emerge.

- Hang in there with what's honest and right even when you have to weather storms for doing so.

- Sometimes those in charge don't see the ethical issue, and even if they do, change doesn't come easily.

"There is a big difference between what we have a right to do and what is right."

—Justice Potter Stewart

III. Doing the Right Thing Often Means More Work

Expediency is a dangerous thing. Edgar learned this lesson eventually, but even before that lesson was clear he found himself studying for tests and doing papers while his friends were acing tests with memory pegs and purchasing term papers. Each time Ari forced Edgar to do the right thing, Edgar had more work to do. Why, there's even another fable going on as Edgar labors away, as his three merry friends enjoy their nights and weekends. It's the fable of the ant and the grasshopper. The ant labors all summer to store food for the winter as the grasshopper plays mightily all summer, only to face starvation in the winter. Edgar labored long and hard, but eventually saw his reward as Drew, Heather, and Steve faced starvation, or at least prison food.

The Story on Extra Work and the Right Thing

Expediency gives you shortcuts that avoid work, but expediency also precludes doing what's right. One of my former students, and my current literary agent, posed the following hypothetical scenario after class one day. Your mother needs an operation without which she will die. She has no money and no insurance. You have no money either, but you are in a position at work where you could take the money. We're talking embezzlement here, not something erudite such as "a temporary transfer of funds for noblesse oblige," or "peer-to-peer funds exchange." He asked if I would take the money to save my mother's life. My simple response was, "No." My student had his own thoughts, "You heartless wench. No wonder I'm getting a 'C' in this class. Why on earth would you answer that question that way?"

My answer was a classic Ari answer, but as physically and mentally abusive as Ari is, he has a soft spot in his heart for his own mother. Stealing the money, which is calling it what it really is, is expedient, but not right. Stealing the money seems noble because we enjoy the crowning glory of taking a fall for our ailing mothers. However, the resolution does not address the issue of what's right. That you avoid more work is not a terribly consistent or effective means for resolving ethical dilemmas.

Begin with the real issues: (1) your mother, a woman you adore, is terribly ill; and (2) you don't steal, a value most mothers teach their children. In resolving to embezzle you place one value above another and ignore the Ari principle that it is neither honest nor right to take funds from another. How do you know that the funds you are taking are not those of a customer who is also ill? Who else is injured by your pilfering?

Put the other value of not stealing into the equation and ask, "Is there another way whereby I can obtain my mother's needs without compromising my values and by doing what's right?" There almost always is. You could pledge everything you own for a loan. You could work out a payment plan with the doctors and hospital. The options involve work, so we feel perfectly justified with the temporary ease of embezzlement because, after all, we were embezzling in the name of something fairly important: a life. A mother's life, no less.

My student's example has far-reaching examples for everyone in business. The *Wall Street Journal*'s Holman W. Jenkins Jr. asked in a column about the Enron executives: "How could they have done it?"[22] His question was along the lines of the Jay Leno classic posed to Hugh Grant when Hugh, who was dating the beautiful Elizabeth

Hurley at the time, was caught by a Hollywood police officer in an automobile with Divine Brown, a, er, shall we say, human relations specialist: "Where was your mind and what were you thinking?" In hindsight we wonder what those who fall off the ethical cliff were thinking at the time they made these decisions. Well, they were thinking, quite rationally, actually, that they were justified in doing what they did. Embezzlement makes perfect sense when you have an ailing mother. And it is the easier of the two alternatives.

This is the skating-by principle, the one that finds all those high school and college students copying each other's homework and finding ways around assignments, studying, and even going to class. The skating-by principle escalates when the skaters hit the work-place. They take their toes right up to the lines of legality and see the big bucks with minimal effort. Lawyers still debate whether Michael Milken broke the law with his carefully crafted finance vehicles. Using the assets of companies he planned to acquire as collateral, he raised the funds for the acquisition through the sale of his infamous junk bonds. It was sort of a sophisticated bet that he could acquire the company and assets or at least get a pay-off from the company's management to go away that would then be used to repay the bond-holders with a handsome return.[23]

Michael Milken rocked the financial world for a time with his highfaluting financial techniques. He and his company eventually experienced the prosecution, the fines, the loss of customers, and the litigation that comes from expedient choices. But for a time they seemed to have it all and so easily, even as we toiled in the trenches.

So it was with Edgar. Edgar slaved away in high school and college and Drew, Heather, and Steve skated through with minimal effort. Expediency could temporarily ease or even eliminate work. But, Ari taught Edgar, and would like you to remember, that the operative word is "temporarily." View the world and your progress looking forward, not sideways to those who are taking the lesser-work and greater-evil approach.

Putting Ari in Action

◆ Don't define ethical issues by using the "either/or" conundrum. There are other options.

◆ Define issues by what's right and what's honest.

◆ Make decisions putting your values first.

◆ Find a way to do what needs to be done without sacrificing honesty or doing something wrong.

◆ Remember that doing what's honest and right will bring more work—but doing what's honest and right also brings the fruits of the extra labor.

"In times like these, it helps to recall that there have always been times like these."

—Paul Harvey

"It is a rough road that leads to the heights of greatness."

—Lucius Annaeus Seneca

IV. Being Ethical Sometimes Means Running Behind in the Race

Centuries ago, Aesop wrote the fable of the tortoise and the hare. In it, the tortoise looks poised to lose the race. But the sprinters often lose precisely because the race is long and they expend too much energy or simply forget to keep at the work required to attain a goal. Appearances are deceptive. Slow but steady can still emerge victorious.

The Story on Running Behind

I've noticed that in January of each year when I am running along the canals, the water-carrying veins of survival here in the Arizona desert, there is a crowd. Fresh from New Year's resolutions, I have plenty of company out there, all in search of fitness. These new fitness buffs, who don't seem to be in particularly good shape, always pass me by, gleefully, making some derogatory comment as they pull ahead, such as, "Pick up the pace, eh?" or "You'll never get in shape that way." I tell you, it hurts. One year there was a fellow wearing one of those hats with a beer can on each side and access straws, like IV lines, pointed toward his mouth. He passed me by. These people are not in shape, but they seem to outrun me and dismay sets in. My thirty-one years of running seem to have all been in vain. Edgar and I are soul mates on these post–New Year's resolution January mornings.

Still, I acknowledge the carefree sprinters with a wave and a smile. Under my breath I mutter, "Wait until July, buddy, when it's 112 in the shade at 5 A.M. We'll see who's running at what speed then." Come July, I am out there alone, the banks of the canal are mine, all mine, because the January athletes are gone, having crashed like meteorites some time between January 1 and January 28, a prime falling-out-of-fitness date.

There is also more to the moral of this canal story. There are certain long-term benefits that accrue that the January athletes can never have. They have speed, but it is temporary and the long-term rewards elude them. For example, any health care worker who has taken my pulse will ask, "Are you a runner?" "Since 1971," I respond.

I hold the fitness benefits that slow and steady running brings to those who hang in there year-round. So it is in business and life. On occasion you will run behind those in the race with you. Do not despair. July and its challenges, not for the fainthearted, are coming. And that slow, steady pace is building strength, endurance, and benefits you won't even realize until decades later.

Let those sprinters pass you by, but take comfort in the fact that Ari and Edgar ran a long and arduous race in which all three friends passed them by on the road to business success. As difficult as it is to watch those sprinters pass you by, let them. Your strength comes from slow and steady endurance built from doing what's honest and right.

As the Enron, WorldCom, and other collapses have come we have seen the fall of some of the great business sprinters of all time. Financial whiz kids such as Andrew Fastow of Enron and Scott Sullivan of WorldCom knocked off our ROI socks for a time. The rest of us were but plodding clods and they were the geniuses. We labored for our pay, and they soared. Well, at least in this part of the story they soared.

Scott Sullivan, the former CFO of WorldCom, and Andrew Fastow, Enron's CFO, are under indictment. Fastow's direct report, Michael Kopper, sang like a canary. Kopper was most distressed about having to surrender the $12 million he made from the off-shore, off-the-books, out-of-this-realm partnerships.[24] The money is gone, federal lockdown awaits, and any hopes of a future CFO position are dreams turned to dust. No one could have been faster on the canals in January than these folks. But July eventually comes to the sprinters who have not done the daily work but try to get ahead with a fast run here and there, but no underlying training and dedication.

Marisa Baridis, age twenty-nine, was the legal compliance officer at Morgan Stanley, Dean Witter, Discover. Her job was to keep information from the deal side of the brokerage house from getting to and being used by the trading side of the house in advance of public disclosures of any of the pending sales, mergers, and acquisitions that involved Morgan Stanley as investment banker. She was in charge of, in Wall Street parlance, the Chinese Wall, that fortress that keeps inside information from flowing through a firm with both a brokerage and investment bank division.[25]

By all accounts, Ms. Baridis did a great job, for Morgan Stanley had a great reputation at that time in terms of its control of advance trading by its brokers. However, the information Ms. Baridis was privy to did take one slight detour from her desk. She was selling the advance information to college friends and others for about $2,500 per tip. She was earning $70,000 per year in salary, but the stock-tip information brought enough money that she could afford a $2,400 per-month Manhattan apartment and a glitzy New York lifestyle. She took in $40,000 extra in one year in the stock-tip business she was conducting on the side. And she saw her lucrative side business as a key to fame, noting for one friend that if their stock-tip scheme ever became public, "We'd be interviewed in every magazine. We'd be in like . . . we'd be, who were the people of the '80s? Boesky? Michael Milken? We'd be bigger than that."[26]

The inside tips that Ms. Baridis doled out to friends for cash, all in $100 bills, brought them advance trades in thirteen companies and $1,000,000 in profits. During the height of the trading activity, Ms. Baridis commented, "It's fun. If you don't get greedy."[27] Plodders looked on in amazement at the gracious, attractive, and cash-rich Baridis. Those who watched the fun from afar, financially and otherwise, perhaps sensed something was amiss but were unable to pinpoint exactly what was happening. Ari would have been nervous. Edgar lived through it and was nervous. The end of the story was coming.

Ms. Baridis didn't quite make it to Boesky fame. The SEC caught up with one of her tippee/brokers, Jeffrey Streich, a thirty-one-year-old who took tips from her over a six-month period. In exchange for leniency, he agreed to wear a wire to meet Ms. Baridis for one last tip. Fully wired, with a camera running across the street, as Streich sat in a Manhattan restaurant window with her, he was nervous. He tried to tip her off without blowing his plea agreement and he asked Ms. Baridis if she understood what they were doing. For the benefit of her prosecutors, who obtained a slam-dunk on intent, she responded, "It's the most illegalist thing you can do."[28]

The feds moved in after seizing the moment and partial confession on tape and took $100,000 in assets Ms. Baridis had accumulated. Her father posted her bail of $250,000. She entered a guilty plea to the federal felony of insider trading and was sentenced to probation in exchange for information on her tippees who were given two to three years.

When you look around and sprinters pass you by mockingly, have faith, dear Ari fan, for the race is not to the swift, but the steady. Steady goes with being honest and doing what's right. The sprinters will fall by the wayside, but the slow and steady prevail.

Putting Ari in Action

- ◆ Let the sprinters pass you by; there's more to the race and more to winning.

- ◆ Don't be enticed by short-term gains.

- ◆ Sprinters falter; don't be discouraged as they pass you by.

"Rancour is an outpouring of a feeling of inferiority."

—Jose Ortega Y Gasset

V. Expect a Little Mockery for Playing Ethically

In the movie *Clear and Present Danger*, Harrison Ford plays his usual Tom Clancy CIA character, Dr. Jack Ryan, who sees issues in black and white and continues to believe without exception that lying is wrong. In one scene, a Washington politico, in response to Ryan's statement that "right" and "wrong" do exist, sneers, "You are such a Boy Scout!"

Not only did Edgar have setbacks, he had to endure the mocking of the temporarily successful around him for his choices on tests, term papers, and even insider trading. Courage is never an easy path and is more difficult because those who choose expediency garner comfort from mocking those taking the more difficult path.

In several of our stories to date, our ethical heroes endured mocking. During the apple juice scandal, plant supervisor Lavery referred to the scientists working for Dr. LiCari as "Chicken Little" and criticized Dr. LiCari publicly and in his evaluations for not being "a team player." Lavery's 1981 evaluation of Dr. LiCari stated that while Dr. LiCari had great technical ability, his judgment was "colored by naiveté and impractical ideals."

The Story on Mockery

The collapse of the FINOVA Group, Inc., a Phoenix-based financial lender, was particularly poignant for me. FINOVA emerged from the stodgy old Greyhound Financial Group in 1992 as a double-digit growth sprinter that had seized the market of smaller business–higher risk lending. Its growth was phenomenal. Its income went from $30.3 million in 1991 to $117 million by 1996 to $13.12 billion by 1999, placing it in the *Forbes* Platinum 400 that same year. It was number twelve on *Fortune's* list of "The 100 Best Companies to Work For." By July of 1999, its stock price had climbed to $54.50 per share and its employees frequently talked of their goal of reaching $60 per share because the company's bonus and incentive plans were tied to that share price. FINOVA enjoyed a debt grade of "A" from both Standard & Poors and Duff & Phelps. FINOVA made it into the *Fortune* 1000 by 1999, and it built new company headquarters in 1999 in Scottsdale, Arizona, at a cost of $50 million.

Everyone wanted to work for FINOVA. The bonus and incentive plans were just part of a package of employee perks that made the rest of the working world envious.[29] Its employees' perks included an on-site gym, tuition benefits of up to $3,000 for children who attended any of the Arizona state universities, free massages, and unlimited time off for volunteer work.[30]

Everyone wanted to be FINOVA. Many looked on from the sidelines or well behind in the race and wondered, "How are they going so fast?" The better question was, "How long can they sprint?"

I was asked by FINOVA executives in 1998 to do an ethical analysis for FINOVA and then present it at a retreat for that team as well as managers from FINOVA operations around the country. When I examined the company I saw a real sprinter, but being a student of Ari's, I am always wary of sprinters.

I did my presentation for the executive team, and I won't say they threw me out of the room, but it was close. Mr. Sam Eichenfeld, then-CEO, laughed out loud at some of the danger signs I discussed with the team. Those were the days when PowerPoint and LCDs were not yet perfected, and there I stood alone with an overhead projector and some slides at the apex of a horseshoe formation of executives telling them that they had a great number of the factors that put them at risk of ethical collapse. (Those forty-five minutes were moments about as tense as any I've ever experienced, and I have been through childbirth four times.) Executives demanded double-digit growth, those who raised accounting issues were quickly transferred or dismissed, the culture was autocratic and sycophantic, and, like Enron, they were spending money as if there were no tomorrow.

I left the room with the officer who was responsible for asking me to do the work and presentation. He was most apologetic. I left and never submitted a bill for my services, so convinced was I that this company was going down. In fact, I wrote it up as my mid-term for my MBA class that spring. My students guffawed at the thought that a company as prominent as FINOVA would ever sink as I was predicting.

But July comes for all sprinters. The day of reckoning comes for all the Steves, Drews, and Heathers of the world. In early 1999, FINOVA had to postpone the release of its annual report. Behind the scenes, FINOVA's auditor, Deloitte & Touche, was objecting to FINOVA's accounting practices for being, at once, overly conservative and overly aggressive. It refused to certify the numbers and Deloitte & Touche was fired.[31]

FINOVA hired Ernst & Young. The annual report was finally issued, but the earnings for 1998 had to be restated before Ernst & Young would certify the financials. A company can survive the write-down of bad loans, even time-sharing resort loans. But when the market begins to doubt the word of the company and managers, investors lose trust and the share price declines. FINOVA began to experience what would be a yearlong descent in its share price. By the end of 1999, its stock price had dipped to $34 per share.[32]

The new year would only bring more bad news because the high-tech economy was also sinking, and in the first quarter FINOVA announced that it would have to write down a $70 million loan to a California computer manufacturer that it had been carrying as an asset when it had become an unassailable proposition that the loan couldn't be collected. The loan as an asset was critical for management bonuses that year. Without it still being carried and not written down, the executive team would not earn its bonuses. The board announced on the same day as the write-down that Eichenfeld was retiring, with a severance package of $10 million.[33]

For those of you keeping financial score, that meant that in one fine day in March 2000, FINOVA took an $80 million hit, for the bad loan and the Eichenfeld compensation package, which amounted to $0.74 per share in one day. And the market was quick to note the hefty ding and took the stock price down to $19.88 from $32 per share.[34] The 38 percent dip in stock value was the largest for any stock on the New York Stock Exchange for March 27, 2000.

The market finally realized the nature of FINOVA's portfolio and its inherent risk. By May 2000, analysts were putting the worth of its portfolio at $0.58 on the dollar.[35] FINOVA's stock price was $12.62 on May 9, 2000. FINOVA lost $1 billion in 2000 and was forced to declare Chapter 11 bankruptcy on March 7, 2001.[36] Its default on its bond debt was the largest since the Great Depression. When it filed bankruptcy, it was the seventh largest bankruptcy in the history of the United States. However, WorldCom and Enron soon joined in and FINOVA slipped down to number nine.[37] One of the great problems with these rankings is that we must rely on these companies' numbers to do the rankings and who knows what their numbers really are!

FINOVA stock would fall to $0.88 per share. FINOVA remains in bankruptcy, a skeleton crew operating what was once a sprinter ahead of nearly all of the pack.

I never heard from FINOVA again after that fateful presentation except for a note from one of FINOVA's officers. He was apologetic about my treatment but wrote in his e-mail to me, "Sam found you ethically rigid." FINOVA never finished the race it began as a first-class sprinter.

Mockery is part of the sprinter's game. My FINOVA experience left me humiliated and possessed of more than a little self-doubt. But, I held firm. Ari taught Edgar to endure the mocking because he knew the outcome. Now so do you. If mockery is coming your way, you perhaps have a fairly good indication that you are doing what's honest and right. In fables and in life, mockery is the precursor to successful completion of the race.

Putting Ari in Action

◆ Expect mockery for doing what's honest and right.

◆ Endure the mockery; this too shall pass.

◆ Garner strength during the mockery from knowing the eventual outcome for the mockers; you will win the race.

⚏

"To sin by silence when they should protest makes cowards of men."

—Abraham Lincoln

"All that is necessary for evil to triumph is for good men to do nothing."

—Edmund Burke

VI. Being Ethical Means You Have to Speak Up

An Ethics Resource Center and Society for Human Resource Management survey revealed that when we do see something illegal or unethical at work we don't do much of anything. The survey indicated that 65 percent of working adults do NOTHING when they see something illegal or unethical at work.[38] When asked why they do nothing, this group had several responses. Ninety-six percent of them said that they chose to do nothing because they feared being accused of "not being a team player." At the heart of many of the ethical debacles in business is generally an employee who tried to let supervisors and the management team know that there was a problem. That employee is, at best, rebuffed, and, at worst, fired. Being accused of "not being a team player" is very much a reality in the battle for organizational ethics.

The most revealing aspect of the survey is that 99 percent of us believe we are the most ethical person in our company. Nearly all of us believe we have higher ethical standards than our coworkers. This perception is wrong but remains important because it reveals that no one is talking about ethics at work. While I would love to meet the 1 percent firmly convinced they are not the most ethical people in the room, I am more concerned about the other 99 percent because they are working in an atmosphere in which they feel helpless to raise ethical standards. Therein lies the problem.

Edgar always feared raising Ari's concerns because he was sure he was the only one in the room who had them. Nothing could be further from the truth. It's the chutzpah thing again. But, here's an Ari thought—saying nothing only makes the fallout worse.

The Story on Speaking Up

At the heart of the scandal that landed the 2002 Winter Olympics in Salt Lake City was an employee who tried to speak up about the bribery she saw taking place.[39] She was fired. Her conscience would not let it rest and she took the story to a local television reporter. The rest, as they say, is history. The Winter Olympics for 2002 will eternally carry the taint of an international bribery scandal. Everyone involved chose to close the deal and land the Olympics. Speaking up might have halted the two speeding luges headed toward each other loaded with reputational damage as well as indictments.

In fairness to Salt Lake City officials and members of that Olympic committee, I do know they were terribly embarrassed by the scandal and the resulting international fallout. In fact, I have noted that they should take some small consolation in knowing that while they may have engaged in bribery, they were very bad at it. An important ethical safety tip is always use cash for bribery, not credit cards or checks, as these officials did. Novices all, at bribery and at understanding that speaking up helps everyone in the long run.

Ethics is a great deal like having an elephant sitting among the desks at your office. We all see the elephant. The elephant, in any place of employment, is truly a problem. But, we don't want to talk about the elephant because it most assuredly means work and difficulties, not to mention the smell. The elephant is a great metaphor because some people have been known to say that ethics stinks.

We allow the elephant to remain, hoping that there are no problems. And most zoo elephants could hang about most industrial firms without wreaking havoc for a time. They might touch a few things on your desk and snatch some items from the lunchroom. They might spray occasionally. These things would be a nuisance, but you could still cohabit with an elephant at work. Ari has noted that elephants have great potential as pookas.

But, despite seeing the elephant and the potential disaster its presence spells, we try to ignore it. Some companies even decorate the elephant by placing a nice fabric wall hanging over it. Hang some plants from the ears and it will be years before zoo auditors catch up with you and the elephant. They do everything they can to avoid resolution of the elephant's presence and hope for the best. After a time, the presence of an elephant does not seem in the least bit odd because the standards for appropriate office occupants have changed.

But that elephant cannot last. Elephants do not fit into cubicles and payroll will have difficulty with the W-2 signatures. The lack of naps alone is going to drive the elephant into a tizzy. When that tizzy comes, there will be destruction in your office and the damages will be far-reaching and perhaps companywide.

Ethics is indeed a great deal like the elephant in the room. When there has been an ethical breach, all those affected will know and see it, but they would just as soon not address it. They will make the ethical problem look better by dressing it up or concealing it from the outside world and regulators. But eventually, the ethical problem explodes and permeates the office and the company. The explosion means the problem is out of control. Everyone then wonders why they didn't act sooner when the elephant was somewhat manageable. Speak up! Ari would want it that way.

Putting Ari in Action

◆ **When you see the issue (elephant), talk to your coworkers.**

◆ **Don't let the elephant go so long that it causes damage.**

◆ The consequences of saying nothing are always greater than
the consequences of speaking up.

##

"Fear knocked at the door. Faith answered. No one was there."

—Old Saying

VII. Sometimes the Ethical Route Is Opportunity Knocking

Doing what's honest and right can be a strategic advantage. Edgar
saw that when he left Steve's company, rather than helping to launch
a defective product. The closed door was just an exit to the resolution of the product problem and a new way to find success in business. If you don't consider doing what's honest and right, you may
develop strategic tunnel vision. You won't see the opportunities that
come from doing what's honest and right because you are too
focused on immediate returns. Ari had to explain to Edgar what
phenomenal opportunities he had in store if he would do what was
honest and right.

The Story on Ethics as an Opportunity

The Johns-Manville Company knew in the 1930s, as reflected in cor-
respondence and board minutes, that asbestos was creating fatal
health problems in the workers in their own factories as well as in
those workers installing or working with asbestos.[40] The company
had everything from irregular autopsies to litigation to scientific

studies that pointed to adverse health effects from asbestos. The company did nothing. In fact, the company even tried to suppress many of the scientific studies and also reached agreements with lawyers for settling one suit in exchange for their agreement not to bring another such suit.[41]

For nearly forty years, Johns-Manville was able to suppress the negative information about asbestos, continue selling it, and maintain earnings. But, when the first product liability suit was appealed and the case was reported, there was a flood of lawsuits that soon buried the company. Johns-Manville was forced into bankruptcy because of the size and number of claims. The bankruptcy ending came about because the company's external auditors refused to sign off on the financial statements. Coopers & Lybrand simply could no longer say the amount the company would owe was "unknowable." To emerge from bankruptcy, Johns-Manville, now just Manville, had to agree to pay 25 percent of its profits in perpetuity to a fund for victims and property restoration.[42] The officers who didn't do what was honest and right had, in effect, made a decision to surrender one-fourth of the company's profits forever.

In the end, when asbestos was outlawed, Johns-Manville was not prepared. It had no substitute product—something that it could and should have developed. Instead, Johns-Manville passed on the strategic opportunities it had if it could have stopped living in denial about the ill-health effects of asbestos. Sometimes by not dealing with the ethical issue, the elephant in the room, or, in this case, the crunch in the lungs, a business develops strategic tunnel vision. The company was so focused on present earnings and sales of asbestos that it forgot to ask questions about the future such as, "What will happen to us when this information about asbestos and our withholding of it becomes public, as it most assuredly will?" In economics parlance, "Assume you will be found out" and take your analysis from there. In strategy parlance, "Is there an opportunity here we're missing?"

Had Manville seized the ethical moment, it could have been developing the new insulation—fiberglass. Opportunity was knocking when its one product developed safety issues. But Johns-Manville did not heed Ari. Seeing its dilemma as strictly an "either/or" that pitted survival against disclosure of the product's harm, Manville failed to see the opportunity to be ahead of the curve on asbestos.

When the three-wheel all-terrain cycles (ATCs) caught the wrath of emergency room physicians because of the spinal cord injuries as well as other severe injuries to children, there was no turning back. Their strong data resulted in a recall of three-wheel cycles by the Consumer Product Safety Commission. The companies that had three-wheelers and were living in denial about their safety were stuck with inventory that could not be sold in the United States. However, there was one company that was poised with a four-wheel ATC, a product that would seize the market.

When the safety issues about the three-wheel ATCs began emerging, most manufacturers attributed the accidents and injuries to "hotdogging," or stunts by riders that were deemed unsafe in the ATC handbooks. They stood firm with the safety of their three-wheelers and their stability. Only one company, Suzuki, designed a four-wheel ATC in response to the safety concerns about the three-wheelers' stability. Suzuki took the data on the safety issues that were creeping upward, percolating to a regulatory head, and, instead of following the industry and living in denial about the unstable elephant in the room, it used the information strategically to offer ATC buffs a safer alternative. Sales were slow until the safety issue came to a boil. With the three-wheel ban, Suzuki's four-wheel ATC was front-and-center and stable and became a wait-listed item.[43] Suzuki seized the ethical moment and conquered the market.

We never know what good things await when we do the right thing. Ari just let Edgar in on them in advance. But the principle holds true even without the promptings of a pooka rabbit.

Putting Ari in Action

◆ See doing what's right and honest as an opportunity, not a burden.

◆ Think through the consequences of right and wrong and explore the opportunities that doing what's right offers.

::

"He giveth power to the faint; and to them that have no might he increaseth strength. . . . they shall run, and not be weary; and they shall walk, and not faint."
—Isaiah 40: 29, 31

VIII. The Ethical Finish First Eventually, and with Peace of Mind

At the end of our story, Edgar is on top of the world even as he sighs after hearing of the mighty falls of his long-time friends. Edgar left the tollbooth behind for a company and success no one could have imagined during all of his setbacks. The ethical do finish first. It just takes time. And their finish is all the more satisfying because there are no federal agents waiting in the wings.

The Story on Eventually Finishing First

In 1982, Tylenol was a $525 million gross earner for McNeil Consumer Products (a division of Johnson & Johnson), with the capsule form of this popular analgesic generating 30 percent of that amount.[44] But within a five-day period, eight people who had used Tylenol capsules purchased in the Chicago area were dead from cyanide poisoning.

A prompt investigation revealed that the poisonings did not occur at the factory because the rapid pace of the production line made it impossible for workers there to taint the capsules. The Food and Drug Administration concluded that the tampering had occurred after the products were on the shelves or during distribution because this was an era in which there were no requirements for tamper-proof packaging. The FDA left the decision to McNeil as to what it would do about the $150 million worth of Tylenol that was already out on store shelves and in the medicine cabinets and homes of consumers.[45]

Law enforcement agencies were fairly confident the tainting was limited to the Chicago area. Inside McNeil, there were the obvious setbacks. $150 million is a tough hit for any company to take. And there were, of course, Bristol-Myers with its Excedrin and American Home Products with Anacin waiting in the wings to seize Tylenol's 40 percent market share.[46] But, McNeil took the hit, risking market share, and hitting its bottom line harder than some of the earnings restatements of 2002. McNeil was playing by the credo of Johnson & Johnson: *primum non nocere.* Above all, do no harm. It's a tough rule that brought them a setback. But, as Edgar would tell them, it's all temporary. Wait, you'll see.

Faced with a financial hit and what was surely perceived as a loss of product goodwill, Tylenol made the recall. But, fast forward to one year after the poisonings, Tylenol's market share was not only what it was before the poisonings, it was higher. Some attribute that change to the tamper-proof packaging. But, no—all of its competitors had tamper-proof packaging as well. Tylenol had earned its extra market share through reputational capital. Tylenol had purchased back its goodwill and then some by agreeing to put its resources on the line when it could not be sure that there were not other tainted capsules out there. Its message was loud and clear, "We will not risk the safety and well-being of our customers for the sake of dollars."

And the poo-pooed CEO Jim Burke, who endured his share of mockery, was cited by then-President Reagan for his ethics, "Jim Burke, of Johnson & Johnson, you have our deepest admiration. In recent days you have lived up to the very highest ideals of corporate responsibility and grace under pressure."[47]

That good reputation carried Tylenol back to its previous market share and then some. The trust that comes from a good reputation goes a long way in business success. Indeed, given some product liability developments with Tylenol over the last few years, many have theorized that Tylenol bought itself immunity from scandal with its $150 million investment. A reputation, good or bad, comes back to help you or it comes back to haunt you. The good one just means you finish first in the long run.

Putting Ari in Action

- ◆ Keep your eyes on your values and doing what's honest and right.

- ◆ Don't be discouraged with the temporary setbacks and costs.

- ◆ Finishing without baggage is the goal.

■■
■■

"What goes around comes around."
—M. M. Jennings' grandmother,
among many others

"Truth percolates."
Mark Helprin

IX. Ethical Indiscretions Haunt the Sprinters

Drew, Heather, and Steve all suffered the consequences for the poor choices they made. It often takes time for the posse to catch up, but it caught up with all three and their demises were not pretty sights. Edgar sighs because of their finales, something he knows they could have avoided if they had chosen the Ari path.

It is the irrefutable principle of "what goes around comes around" that should provide the courage for saying, "No," with or without a rabbit pooka. And with this very scientific principle, one can make a convincing case to many people to do what's honest and right.

Many have told me that it is impossible to teach ethics to graduate students. My standard response is, "Perhaps so, but you can teach fear." The fear of getting caught is a powerful motivator for those who have not had Ari or progressed upward on the scale of moral development.

Missteps and misdeeds surface, sometimes years later, as we learned with Drew, Steve, and Heather. Novelist Mark Helprin has noted that truth is like a natural force that must percolate to the surface. It cannot be bound. So the embarrassing aspects of our lives, deals, and operations slowly but surely come to the surface.

One of Dostoyevsky's observations in *Crime and Punishment* is that lying is good; it is the only way we ever get at the truth. His simple observation is profound. When it comes to recalling events we are very able when our minds are focused on what actually happened. If we have substituted something for the truth, our minds cannot recall everything that we have said and inconsistencies develop.

Our misdeeds and missteps come to light because we are incapable of maintaining the front of a falsehood. Mark Twain once said, "Always tell the truth. That way you don't have to remember anything." We simply don't have the mental skill to maintain two different stories about our conduct or an event. The inconsistencies pop through because truth is one stubborn force.

The moment of truth is that point in time when a person or company realizes that something is awry with their product, practices, earnings statements, or culture. The moment of truth has very bad timing. It usually comes when things are peachy in sales and earnings. Without an Ari around, the tendency is to launch the product, give the stock tip, or cook the books.

Knowing the inevitable outcome—for truth does percolate—why do bright and experienced people ignore the moment of truth and continue to hope they can keep it under wraps? You can't suppress the truth. Circumstances beyond even the best manager's control take over once the moment of truth has passed. The Hell's Angels (and Ari has great regard for their common sense) have it right, "Three people can keep a secret if two are dead."

The Story on Haunting Truth

Dianna Green had enjoyed a remarkable career, rising through the ranks at Duquesne Light to the position of senior vice president, a woman with an MBA, experience, and business savvy. Then a former employee filed suit against the company and Ms. Green was deposed by the employee's lawyer. During routine background questions, Ms. Green hesitated in providing the attorney with the date and institution for the MBA degree listed as part of her credentials.

The attorney for the employee checked with the institution Ms. Green had named and discovered that she indeed had no degree. When he notified Duquesne executives, they negotiated a severance package with her and announced that she was leaving the company to pursue "other career interests."[48] While she perhaps felt that she needed the falsified MBA to get her promotion to the executive ranks, she was, by all accounts, an extremely capable and hard worker. She was on the board of directors of Pennsylvania's largest bank and was a tireless servant in community organizations in Pittsburgh. Her achievements spoke for themselves. Unfortunately, she didn't let them and the false resume came to light in a deposition, circumstances beyond her control. Tragically, Ms. Green, also coping with her own diabetes and family illnesses, took her own life shortly after leaving her position at Duquesne.

In 1973, General Motors was poised to launch a new look for its old Malibu, a mid-size car in its Chevy line. Prior to the ramp up of production, a low-level engineer, Edward C. Ivey, wrote an internal memo on "value analysis" for "post-collision fuel-tank fires" in the Malibu. Mr. Ivey explained in the memo that it would cost about $2.40 per car to fix what he was describing as a gas tank positioned too close to the rear bumper of the new design with insufficient cushion. His fear was that the car would explode upon rear-end impact, even at lower speeds. Those of you of another generation will recognize that history repeats. Ford experienced a similar memo from one of its engineers prior to its launch of the Ford

Pinto, America's first response to the small, fuel-efficient Japanese competition.[49]

Young Mr. Ivey's memo explained that there could be lost life, and he valued human life at $200,000, even as he apologized noting that "it is really impossible to put a value on human life."[50] He proposed taking steps to curb the fuel-fed fires that might result from rear-end collisions involving the Malibu. Despite the memo and young Ivey's concerns, the new Malibu went forward into production and respectable sales.

In 1981, as litigation on the rear-end collisions began, an in-house lawyer uncovered the Ivey memo, another moment of truth and a good time to let the ethical indiscretion be known as to prevent any further harm. Instead, the in-house lawyer wrote yet another memo with this warning:

> Obviously Ivey is not an individual whom we would ever, in any conceivable situation, want identified to the plaintiffs in a post-collision fuel-fed fire case, and the documents he generated are undoubtedly some of the potentially most harmful and most damaging were they ever to be produced.[51]

On Christmas Eve 1993, Patricia Anderson, her four children, and a friend, Jo Tigner, were rear-ended in their Chevy Malibu by a drunk driver who had a blood-alcohol level of .20 and was traveling at a speed of 70 mph. Those in the car who were not killed were severely burned and disfigured as a result of a fuel-fed fire springing from the gas tank.

Mrs. Anderson and others filed suit against GM, and her lawyers came across both the Ivey memo and the in-house lawyer's follow-up to that memo. The judge in the case admitted these two documents, which became critical for the jury in its deliberation and the award of $4.8 billion, later reduced to $1.2 billion.[52] Also, the judge refused to allow evidence of the driver's speed or blood-alcohol level. The result was that Coleman Thorton, the foreman of the jury, explained the size of the verdict as follows, "GM has no regard for the people in their cars, and they should be held responsible for it."[53] A few moments of truth passed by, and the result is, nearly thirty years later, $1.2 billion. Ford was indicted in Indiana for negligent homicide and paid hundreds of millions in damages for its Pinto.

It's simply a matter of time before truth percolates. Ari would be quick to point out that even Drew's high school antics came back to haunt him come sentencing time. Fear begets fortitude, and the fear of ethical and legal problems emerging is a very real and a very certain thing.

Putting Ari in Action

◆ Always tell the truth; that way you don't have to worry or remember.

◆ When facing a moment of truth, disclose and move on.

◆ Remember the freedom of not being haunted by a falsehood.

"A bad reputation is like a hangover. It takes a while to get rid of and it makes everything else hurt."
—James Preston, former CEO, Avon

"A reputation, good or bad, is tough to shake."
—Richard Teerlink, CEO, Harley Davidson

X. Success Comes from Doing What's Honest and Right

Edgar learned from Ari not to be so busy aiming for success that you fail to see that success comes from doing what's honest and right. Doing what's honest and right is a business strategy, an opportunity. And most poor schmucks fail to see this sure-fire path to success. The beauty of ethics is that it's available to everyone as a strategy. Most reject it out of hand and miss out on its grand rewards.

The Story on Success

Sherron Watkins, the executive at Enron who wrote the memo pleading with the company to come clean on its accounting, knew she was making a career move. And it looked for a time as if her career was over and done at Enron.[54] It was, whether Enron survived or tanked. But doing what was honest and right has brought her a lucrative book contract, speaking engagements, and a whole new career. She perhaps didn't realize she was ending a bad career in exchange for a different, dynamic, and more peaceful one.

Over the last two years, I have undertaken the task of remodeling my two-decade-old home. Were I to offer advice on this process to those contemplating it, it would be simply, "Don't. Just move." However, if you are of a mind to remodel, what I learned may help.

I learned over the course of many contractors, much expense, and enormous frustration that there are very few folks in the construction industry who don't lie to you about cost, time, completion, and even what Taco Bell has on special that day. And by the end of the two-year process I found that I was hiring those contractors whose bids were not always the lowest. From an economic perspective one has to wonder why. I chose them because I had used them before and they kept their word. I came to value honesty among contractors. That I paid a bit more was not a problem, because I saved in the long run with the lack of extra phone calls, time, and motels for the nights when deadlines were not met. It was the honest contractors who earned and retained my business.

Many contractors saw telling us the little white lie of promising they would be done "in two weeks" as a means of obtaining my business. Instead, they sealed their competitive fate. Those who lied have lost at least ten referrals to my neighbors because they were not honest with me. They sacrificed ten jobs to get one. A quick sprint to a contract. A loss over the long term. A tiny indiscretion that costs them the race. Edgar sighs because he saw what Drew's, Steve's, and Heather's failure to see ethics as an opportunity cost them. Ari provided the ability to see ethics in a different light: a true strategic advantage in business.

Putting Ari in Action

- **View ethics not as a deterrent but an opportunity for success.**
- **Remember the race has a nonlinear path and you may lose some opportunities if you fail to see what's right and honest as a means for succeeding.**

Rabbit Redux: Putting Ari in Action

Ari is there with us all. We know his familiar pummel because we keep feeling something is not quite right about a decision, a statement, or an action. If you respond to Ari's irritations, he hangs with you until he is a part of you. Ignore him and, well, you become Mrs. Vera Benchley or, worse, Andrew Fastow, Scott Sullivan, or Bernie Ebbers. You lose that sensitivity to what's honest and what's right. And doing both is the key to winning the race. Let them pass you by temporarily. Take those setbacks. Endure the mockery. What awaits you is success you could not have imagined as you took the hard path at the fork in the road when what was honest and what was right seemed much too much to ask of anyone. Just do it. Make Ari proud.

Notes

1. Paul Singer, "Business Schools Push Ethics Training," *Arizona Republic*, August 26, 2002, D1, D3.

2. Anita Raghavan, Kathryn Kranhold, and Alexei Barrionuevo, "How Enron Bosses Created a Culture of Pushing Limits," *Wall Street Journal*, August 26, 2002, A1, A7.

3. Jonathan Weil and Alexei Barrionuevo, "Justice Department Finds Building Criminal Case Against Lay Tough," *Wall Street Journal*, August 26, 2002, A3, A7.

4. Matt Krantz, "Peeling Back the Layers of Enron's Breakdown," *USA Today*, January 22, 2002, 2B.

5. *Ibid.*

6. At this point, it would be a good idea to note that Michael J. Kopper, a lieutenant to Enron's CFO, Andrew Fastow, entered a guilty plea to mail and wire fraud in exchange for singing like a canary about his former bosses. Kurt Eichenwald, "Ex-Enron Official Admits Payments to Finance Chief," *New York Times*, August 22, 2002, A1, C6.

7. *www.josephsoninstitute.org.*

8. Cheryl Wetstein, "Lying, Cheating Has Become Widespread Among Teens," *Washington Times*, October 23–29, 2000, pp. 1 and 23.

9. "Executives Pad Resumes," *USA Today*, October 16, 2001, 1B.

10. Deborah Parrish, "The Scientific Misconduct Definition and Falsification of Credentials," *Professional Ethics Report*, Fall 1996, 9(4), pp. 1 and 6. See also S. V. Gurudevan and W. R. Mower, "Misrepresentation of Research Publications Among Emergency Medicine Residency Applicants," *Annals of Emergency Medicine*, 27(3) (1996), pp. 327–330.

11. *The KPMG 2000 Organizational Integrity Survey: A Summary* (2000); available at www.uskpmg.com/main.html.

12. Dawn Blalock, "Study Shows Many Execs Are Quick to Write Off Ethics," *Wall Street Journal,* March 26, 1996, pp. C1, C22.

13. *Ibid.*

14. Shannon Reilly and Robert Ahrens, "Business Executives Rate Honesty," *USA Today*, May 28, 2002, p. 1B.

15. Del Jones, "Many CEOs Bend the Rules (of Golf)," *USA Today,* June 25, 2002, pp. 1A and 2A.

16. *Ibid.*

17. *Ibid.*

18. Chris Welles, "What Led Beech-Nut Down the Road to Disgrace," *BusinessWeek,* February 22, 1988, pp. 124–128.

19. Except as otherwise noted, the facts are taken from the series of cases involving the criminal prosecution of the officers involved: *U.S. v. Beech-Nut, Inc.*, 871 F.2d 1181 (2nd Cir. 1989); 925 F.2d 604 (2nd Cir. 1991); *cert. denied,* 493 U.S. 933 (1989).

20. Chris Welles, "What Led Beech-Nut Down the Road to Disgrace," *BusinessWeek,* February 22, 1988, pp. 124–128.

21. *U.S. v. Beech-Nut, Inc.,* 871 F.2d 1181.

22. Holman W. Jenkins Jr., "How Could They Have Done It?" *Wall Street Journal,* August 28, 2002, A15.

23. Dorothy Rabinowitz, "Unpardoned," *Wall Street Journal,* February 13, 2001, A 26.

24. Kurt Eichenwald, "Ex-Enron Official Admits Payments to Finance Chief," *New York Times,* August 22, 2002, A1, C6.

25. Dean Starkman, "Five Brokers Indicted for Insider Trades Linked to

Ex–Morgan Stanley Officer," *Wall Street Journal*, December 23, 1997, p. B9.

26. Elise Ackerman, "Remember Boesky? Many Gen Xers Don't," *U.S. News & World Report*, November 22, 1999, p. 52.

27. Peter Truell, "Lessons of Boesky and Milken Go Unheeded in Fraud Case," *New York Times*, November 26, 1997, pp. C1, C10.

28. Dean Starkman, "Three Indicted for Insider Trading Tied to Ex–Morgan Stanley Aide," *Wall Street Journal*, November 26, 1997, p. B2.

29. Dawn Gilbertson, "Finova's Perks Winning Notice," *Arizona Republic*, December 22, 1998, pp. E1, E8.

30. "The 100 Best Companies to Work For," *Fortune*, January 11, 1999, p. 122.

31. Dawn Gilbertson, "Finova Record Smudged," *Arizona Republic*, April 18, 1999, pp. D1, D2.

32. Max Jarman, "Finova Group's Stock Sinks," *Arizona Republic*, December 10, 1999, pp. E1, E2.

33. *Ibid.*

34. *Ibid.*

35. Donna Hogan, "Finova Finances May Force Sale," *Tribune*, May 9, 2000, pp. B1, B2.

36. Max Jarman, "Finova Posts $1 Billion Loss," *Arizona Republic*, April 3, 2001, p. D1.

37. www.bankruptcydata.com.

38. The study was conducted by the Ethics Resource Center and the Society for Human Resource Management. The study can be found at www.shrm.org or www.ethics.org.

39. Jo Thomas, Kirk Johnson, and Jere Longman, "From an Innocent Bid to Olympic Scandal," *New York Times*, March 17, 1998, pp. A1, A15.

40. Paul Brodeur, "The Asbestos Industry on Trial," *New Yorker*, June 10, 1985, p. 64; June 17, 1985, p. 69; June 24, 1985, p. 62; and July 1, 1985, p. 63. The material from the *New Yorker* series became a book, *Outrageous Misconduct: The Asbestos Industry on Trial* by Paul Brodeur (New York: Pantheon Books, 1985).

41. *Ibid.*

42. Wade Lambert and Ellen Joan Pollock, "Manville to Add Funds to Asbestos Trust," *Wall Street Journal*, September 10, 1990, p. B11.

43. "Outlawing a Three-Wheeler," *Time,* January 11, 1988, p. 59.

44. "The Tylenol Rescue," *Newsweek*, March 3, 1986, p. 52.

45. "Drug Firm Pulls All Its Capsules Off the Market," *Arizona Republic*, February 18, 1986, A2.

46. "The Tylenol Rescue," *Newsweek*, March 3, 1986, p. 52.

47. *Ibid.*

48. Carol Hymowitz and Raju Narisetti, "A Promising Career Comes to a Tragic End, and a City Asks Why," *Wall Street Journal*, May 9, 1997, pp. A1, A8.

49. Rachel Dardis and Claudia Zent, "The Economics of the Pinto Recall," *Journal of Consumer Affairs,* Winter 1982, pp. 261-277.

50. Milo Geyelin, "How an Internal Memo Written 26 Years Ago Is Costing GM Dearly," *Wall Street Journal*, September 29, 1999, pp. A1, A6.

51. *Ibid.*

52. Margaret A. Jacobs, "BMW Decision Used to Whittle Punitive Awards," *Wall Street Journal*, September 13, 1999, p. B2.

53. Ann W. O'Neill, Henry Weinstein, and Eric Malnic, "Jury Orders GM to Pay Record Sum," *Arizona Republic*, July 10, 1999, pp. A1, A2.

54. Michael Duffy, "What Did They Know and When Did They Know It?" *Time*, January 28, 2002, pp. 16-27.

Index

About the Author

Professor Marianne M. Jennings served as director of the Joan and David Lincoln Center for Applied Ethics from 1995 to 1999 at Arizona State University. For the past twenty-five years, she has taught legal and ethical studies to business students.

She has appeared on *CBS This Morning*, the *Today Show*, and the *CBS Evening News*. Her weekly columns are syndicated around the country, and her work has appeared in the *Chicago Tribune*, the *Wall Street Journal*, the *New York Times*, the *Washington Post*, and *Reader's Digest*. She was given an Arizona Press Club award in 1994 for her work as a feature columnist and has been a commentator for business issues on *All Things Considered* for National Public Radio.

Professor Jennings has worked with the Federal Public Defender and U.S. Attorney in Nevada and has done consulting work for law firms, businesses, and professional groups including IBM, Dial Corporation, Motorola, the National Association of Credit Managers, Mesa Community College, Southern California Edison, the Arizona Auditor General, Midwest Energy Supply, Hy-Vee Foods, Bell Helicopter, Amgen, VIAD, and the Cities of Phoenix, Mesa, and Tucson.

Professor Jennings earned her undergraduate degree in finance and her J.D. from Brigham Young University. She has authored more than 130 articles in academic, professional, and trade journals. Currently, she has six textbooks and monographs in circulation. In 2000, the *New York Times* MBA Pocket Series published her book on corporate governance, *Boards of Directors*.

Jennings conducts countless workshops and seminars in the areas of business, personal, government, legal, academic, and professional ethics that provide a great outlet for book sales. She has been named Professor of the Year in the College of Business in 1981, 1987, and 2000 and was the recipient of a Burlington Northern teaching excellence award. She was named a Wakonse Fellow in 1994 and was named Distinguished Faculty Researcher for the College of Business that same year. She has been a Dean's Council of 100 Distinguished Scholars since 1995. In 1999, she was given best-article awards by the Academy of Legal Studies in Business and the Association for Government Accountants, and in 2000, the Association of Government Accountants inducted her into its Speakers Hall of Fame.

She is a contributing editor for the *Real Estate Law Journal* and the *Corporate Finance Review*. She has received nine research grants. In 1984, she served as then-Governor Bruce Babbitt's appointee to the Arizona Corporation Commission. From 1986 to 1987, she served as ASU's faculty athletic representative to the NCAA and PAC-10. During 1986–1988, she served as associate dean in the College of Business. In 1999, she was appointed by Governor Jane Dee Hull to the Arizona Commission on Character and elected president of the Arizona Association of Scholars.

Professor Jennings is a member of twelve professional organizations, including the State Bar of Arizona, and has served on four boards of directors, including that of Arizona Public Service from 1987 to 2000.